you are™ what you eat

you are what you eat™

Live Well, Live Longer

Compiled by
Carina Norris, MSc RNutr

TED SMART

First published in Great Britain in 2007 by
Virgin Books Ltd
Thames Wharf Studios
Rainville Road
London
W6 9HA

This edition produced for The Book People,
Hall Wood Avenue, Haydock, St Helens, WA11 9UL

A catalogue record for this book is available from the British Library.

ISBN 978 07535 1291 3

The paper used in this book is a natural, recyclable product made from wood grown in sustainable forests. The manufacturing process conforms to the regulations of the country of origin.

Designed by Virgin Books Ltd
Printed and bound in Italy

Every effort has been made to ensure that the information in this book is accurate. The information in this book will be relevant to the majority of people but may not be applicable in each individual case so it is advised that professional medical advice is obtained for specific health matters. Neither the publisher nor Celador accept any legal responsibility for any personal injury or other damage or loss arising from the use of misuse of the information in this book. Anyone making a change in their diet should consult their GP especially if pregnant, infirm, elderly or under 16.

Recipe photography courtesy of Salton Europe/Russell Hobbs
Food and lifestyle images copyright © Shutterstock, except pages 209, 211, 214 copyright © Corbis.

Contents

Welcome to You Are What You Eat: Live Well, Live Longer

you are™
what
you eat™

Introduction

Eating well really can change your life. Not just the way you look (though it can certainly do that) but, more importantly, the way you feel. Good, nutritious food can give you energy, boost your mood and even increase your life expectancy. A healthy diet and lifestyle is the closest thing you'll find to a fountain of youth!

You Are What You Eat™ is all about helping people to enjoy eating the foods that will make them feel great. It's simple – eat junk, and you'll feel rotten. But feed yourself nutritious fuel, and you can feel like a million dollars!

'Nutritionists and doctors are learning more and more about how the food we eat affects our resistance to disease'

As the title of this book says, healthy eating can help you to live *well*. Nutritious, tasty food will give you bags of energy, enabling you to live life to the full. A good diet will help you maintain a sensible weight (and lose weight if you need to), which, as well as being healthy, is a great self-esteem booster. Staying on the subject of mood, nutrition can help you to stay upbeat, and protect you from mood swings and depression. Poor nutrition quickly leads to low-grade nutritional deficiencies, which may not cause overt symptoms, but make you feel low and off-colour. Good nutrition, on the other hand, boosts your immune system, so your body is better able to take any stresses and damage the world throws at it, and fight off the bugs and germs that attack us every day.

So, we know that eating well helps us to live *well*. It also helps us to live *longer*. Nutritionists and doctors are learning more and more about how the food we eat affects our resistance to disease. Some foods – saturated fats, refined sugars and salt are good examples – promote your risk of serious chronic conditions such as high blood pressure, clogged arteries, type-2 diabetes, heart disease and cancer, all diseases that can take years off your life. But by cutting down on these nutritional nasties, and increasing the health-promoting foods, you can add years to your life.

What are these 'live longer' nutrients and foods? You'll learn all about them in *You Are What You Eat: Live Well, Live Longer,* but here's just a taster . . . Fruits and vegetables are rich in vitamins, minerals and natural plant chemicals that reduce your risk of all the big killer diseases. Nuts and seeds are full of heart-healthy oils and immune-boosting antioxidants. And low-fat dairy products will help build and maintain strong bones, and may even help you get to and maintain a healthy weight.

Healthy eating to live long and well needn't be a chore – you won't have to chew your way through meals that taste of sawdust, or spend hours in the kitchen or a fortune on obscure ingredients. If you think life wouldn't be worth living without the occasional chocolate, fear not! Healthy eating *isn't* about deprivation, it's about moderation. You *are* allowed treats – in fact, they're vital.

And food isn't the whole story – once you revamp the rest of your lifestyle you'll *really* start to feel the benefits. Fuel your body with nutritious food, cut out the junk and the bad habits (we're talking things like smoking and overindulging in alcohol here) that slow you down and sap your get-up-and-go, and you'll have plenty of energy and enthusiasm for all the exercise you said you 'weren't up to' or 'didn't have time for' before. Combining eating well with plenty of activity is a sure-fire recipe for feeling great. It'll also maximise your potential for a long, healthy life.

This book can benefit everyone, whatever their age, with quizzes and tailored advice and tips for the whole family, from young children to sprightly seniors. We're not going to blind you with science, but we will give you the nutritional know-how to make the healthy choices that will help you reap the benefits. And we'll make it easy – with plenty of practical advice and hints to get everyone on board and enjoying their new way of eating. Whether you've got a picky five-year-old, a teenager with a serious crisp habit, a husband who refuses to eat 'rabbit food', or just a desire to get into last year's jeans, this book can help!

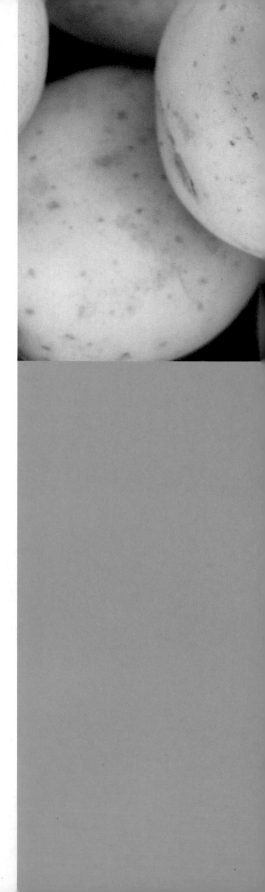

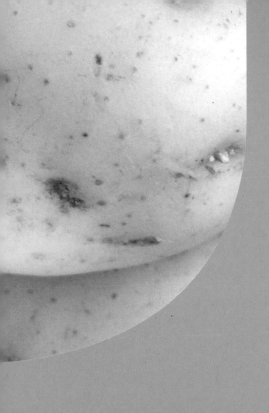

All of our advice is realistic – what's the point of a healthy eating and lifestyle plan you can't stick to because it takes too much time, costs a fortune or leaves you hungry? This isn't a fad diet – it's a new way of eating that's practical, sustaining and tasty.

Redefining your diet can change your life, whatever your age, but the sooner you begin the better. So, although this book is divided into three different 'Lifestages', we're not intending that you wait until you get to those ages before reading the sections!

HOW TO USE THIS BOOK

Through our lives, our nutritional needs change, and so do our health concerns. For example, a healthy diet for a small child, who is growing very rapidly, is very different to that for her father, who may work as a gardener, or her grandmother, who may suffer from osteoporosis.

So this book is divided into three sections, each looking at a different Lifestage, the nutrients needed, and different health issues that are most likely to arise at that time.

Lifestage 1:   5–25
Lifestage 2:   25–50
Lifestage 3:   50+

In each Lifestage section, you'll find plenty of practical advice – tips and recipes to enable you to incorporate the *Live Well, Live Longer* benefits into your busy life.

We'll also tackle the 'Five Big Issues' that affect all of us, and can be addressed through diet.
- Weight gain – how to shed excess pounds without pain
- Immunity and resisting disease – eat to beat the bugs, and fend off chronic diseases
- Digestion problems – learn to be good to your gut
- Stress – what to eat when the going gets tough
- Hormones – eat to beat PMS, smooth out the menopause and boost your mood

Of course, healthy eating is a long-term thing, not a quick fix or a fad diet, and good nutrition in childhood sets the groundwork for a healthy adult life. The earlier you start eating to beat the chronic diseases that generally strike later in life, such as heart disease and stroke, the better the chances are they'll pass you by.

For example, youngsters who eat a diet rich in calcium and vitamin D and take plenty of exercise in childhood and adolescence will build up the maximum deposit in their 'bone bank'. And the sooner you reduce the amount of unhealthy fat and salt in your diet, the better your chances of keeping your heart and blood vessels healthy your whole life long.

Lifestage 1 is still relevant after you've passed 25 – you may have children of your own. The advice in Lifestage 2 is full of useful advice and information, even if that stage of your life is in the past or the future. And the third Lifestage section isn't only intended for people who've reached the age of fifty, it's all about conditions and issues that generally arise during that time of your life. So, for example, while the bone-thinning disease osteoporosis usually doesn't develop until the senior years (and so is covered in Lifestage 3), the sooner you start building up your bones by eating plenty of calcium-rich foods, the more likely you are to stay strong, fit and healthy into old age.

It's never too early to smarten up your diet – anyone can reap the benefits in terms of better health and vitality. Saying 'I've got to the age I am without any problems – why should I change?' is not an option! Anyone can improve their health, and even add years to their life, just by changing their eating habits for the better.

Your energy levels and immunity will improve from day one. And over the following weeks, your mood will stabilise, and any excess weight you've been carrying will gradually fall away.

You've got nothing to lose, and everything to gain – what are you waiting for?

'It's never too early to smarten up your diet – anyone can reap the benefits in terms of better health and vitality'

How To Live Well Fuel For Life

People often talk about food being 'fuel' for your body, like petrol for a car. And in a way, it's a good analogy – food gives you energy and keeps you going. And, you need the right fuel to get the best performance. You wouldn't put poor-quality fuel into an expensive sports car, so you shouldn't feed your body on junk food – you're worth much more than the flashiest set of wheels!

But food is more than just fuel. Good food impacts on every aspect of our health and wellbeing – every system in our body, from our heart and lungs to our brain, bones and muscles. Nutritious food even helps us to look our best, keeping our skin, teeth and hair in tiptop condition.

Food is for:
1. Growth and repair – building and maintaining a healthy body
2. Living and doing – fuel for life
3. Protection and performance – defence against stress, injury and disease, enabling your body to function at its best

Different nutrients serve different purposes, and some have many roles. But you don't need to learn long lists of vitamins and minerals in order to eat well and feed your family healthily. All you need to know is which foods make up a healthy diet – what to choose and what to avoid – and that's really not complicated.

And food isn't just about maintaining your body and giving you energy to live, it's about enjoyment too! Thank heavens the science fiction writers' prediction of everyone just popping a nutrient pill every morning never came to pass – life would be a pretty joyless affair without good food!

Healthy food can be delicious, and occasionally you can have a small amount of less healthy food – you just have to be sensible about it. Far better to allow yourself to 'relax' a little sometimes than let your diet take over your life and make you hung up and anxious about nutrition.

If you're clued up and well informed, you can make the healthy choices, and that's where this book comes in. And because the food we're recommending is tasty, varied and easy to prepare, you'll enjoy eating it, so you'll be far more likely to stick to your new, healthier way of eating. In time, you'll probably find you don't enjoy the less healthy foods so much. You'll find your sweet tooth is less sharp, greasy food just makes you feel heavy and bloated, and too much caffeine gives you the jitters.

You might also think that we're allowing you to eat an awful lot of food. That's because most foods in a healthy diet are 'nutrient dense', that means packed with goodness. Many of the foods you'll be cutting down or out – things like junk food, fizzy drinks and fatty snacks – are 'energy dense', and packed with calories! So, you can eat more of the good foods than the bad foods, and still not put on weight, which can't be bad!

You can also have lots of meals – but they might be smaller than you're used to. Eating little and often helps keep your energy levels nice and stable, making you less likely to grab a chocolate bar or packet of crisps to tide you over until the next meal. Smaller meals also prevent that 'stuffed to bursting' feeling after big meals that can upset your body's own natural 'fullness' receptors. When it comes to healthy eating, grazing is better than gorging. If you don't habitually eat too much at a sitting, you'll be more in tune with your body's energy needs, and less likely to overeat at any time.

Try to organise your eating around the following meals and snacks:

- Breakfast (eaten soon after you get up)
- Mid-morning snack
- Lunch
- Mid-afternoon snack
- Supper
- Bedtime drink and snack (optional)

Eating three meals and a couple of healthy snacks each day fits in with most of our lifestyles, though obviously some people may find it easier to have their main meal in the middle of the day, while for others an evening main meal is the best option.

EVERY DAY DESERVES A GOOD START

Most people know that breakfast is one of the most (if not the most) important meals of the day, but studies have found that one in four Britons – adults and children – regularly give it a miss. A lot of women still believe that skipping breakfast is a useful dieting strategy, but it isn't. Research has proved that those missing out on this vital fuel boost are likely to more than make up for it calorie-wise during the day.

Eating a healthy breakfast every day is, in fact, a way of keeping your healthy eating on track and helping you to lose or control your weight. Kick-start your body with a nutritious breakfast and you're less likely to reach for the biscuit tin or that chocolate bar lurking in your desk.

TIME FOR LUNCH

Give yourself a nutrient and energy top-up at lunchtime by ensuring that your meal includes some wholemeal bread or other wholegrains, a portion of protein and as many vegetables as you can. It's also an opportunity to make a contribution to your 5-a-day by including a piece of fruit.

EVENING MEAL

If you prefer your main meal in the evening, try to eat as early as you can to allow time to digest your food before bedtime.

SNACK TIME

Remember, snacks are mini-meals, so be sensible about your choices. Fruit, some vegetable sticks and a low-fat dip, a couple of oatcakes spread with a little low-fat cream cheese, a handful of low-fat pretzels, nuts and dried fruit, or plain popcorn are ideal to stave off between-meal munchies. Carefully chosen, snacks are also an opportunity to top up your energy-giving starchy carbohydrates and your intake of valuable fruit and vegetables.

MAKE TIME TO EAT TOGETHER

Making time for family meals, whenever possible, has more benefits than you may think. Not only do they strengthen the family bonds and help you keep track of everyone's lives, research has found that they actually improve mental and physical health.

'Remember, snacks are mini-meals, so be sensible about your choices'

A recent study by the University of Minnesota showed that children from families who sat down to dinner together almost every day ate more healthily, consuming higher amounts of important nutrients such as fibre, calcium, iron and vitamins B6, B12, C and E. They also consumed less fat than children from families who never or only occasionally ate together.

Children who ate family meals also consumed more fruit, vegetables and fewer snack foods than children who ate their meals separately.

FAMILY MEALS – KEEP IT SIMPLE

Getting everyone together for family meals isn't always easy, particularly if you're rushing home from work, loading the washing machine, collecting children from after-school activities and racing round the supermarket. But the benefits make it well worthwhile.

Family meals don't have to be evening meals. They could be breakfasts or weekend lunches, whatever fits in best with your busy schedule. Keep the meals simple, and get everyone to help.

Foods For Growth And Repair

PROTEIN

Everyone needs protein to build new cells and replace those that are damaged or worn out. Fortunately in this country, getting enough protein is rarely a problem – the issue is where we get it from!

Most people need to concentrate more on the quality of their protein than the amount. In fact, eating excessive protein is pointless, and can lead to health problems. Protein can be divided into:

● **Animal protein** – meat, fish, eggs, dairy products
● **Vegetable protein** – pulses (beans and lentils), nuts, seeds and wholegrains, tofu and soya products

Animal protein is easier for the body to use, but it's higher in fat, especially the unhealthy saturated fat (but more about that later). Vegetarian food is lower in fat (and calories) and higher in fibre, but harder for the body to use. Both are good sources of different vitamins and minerals.

Unless you're a vegetarian, it's probably best to get your protein from as wide a variety of sources as possible, making sure to choose the low-fat versions of animal proteins.

POULTRY

Chicken is a great source of protein, and turkey's too good to save just for Christmas! They're both lower in fat (especially saturated fat) than red meat, extremely versatile, and also supply good amounts of B-vitamins, and the minerals zinc and selenium, both important for immunity.

 **Live well tip**
Skin that bird – remove the skin before cooking poultry, as that's where most of the fat lurks.

'Chicken is a great source of protein, and turkey's too good to save just for Christmas!'

Duck is higher in iron than 'paler' poultry, but it's also much higher in fat – over 10g of fat per 100g, compared with approximately 2g per 100g for chicken.

MEAT

Red meats like beef, lamb and pork are high in protein and iron – but the flip side is their high saturated-fat content. If you like your meat, gain the nutritional benefits and minimise the disadvantages by:

● Not eating red meat too often – stick to once or twice a week maximum
● Always trimming off the fat
● Using low-fat cooking methods, such as grilling, braising, casseroling or roasting, rather than frying
● Buying cuts of meat to mince yourself – bought mince often has a lot of fat 'minced in'
● Avoiding processed meats (see box)

MEAT, POULTRY AND FISH – WHAT TO AVOID

Cook quality meat yourself, rather than relying on processed foods – they're generally much higher in fat and salt, and padded out with water and artificial fillers.

Give these processed proteins a miss:
● Burgers (except for those you make yourself)
● Sausages and sausage rolls
● Salami and other 'fancy sausages'
● Scotch eggs
● Pork pies
● Black pudding and white pudding
● Chicken nuggets (except for home-made, or those made from chicken breast in a low-fat, low-salt coating)
● Re-formed meat slices (these are made from low-quality minced-up meat, re-formed and sliced) – look for meat just labelled 'sliced' – then you know it hasn't been processed
● Re-formed chicken and fish 'shapes' for children
● Deep-fried fish

FISH

Fish is a fantastically nutritious food – we really ought to eat more of it! All fish is high in protein, and rich in the minerals zinc and selenium (needed for strong immune defences), and iodine (for healthy functioning of the thyroid gland). It's also a source of B-vitamins.

Fish is divided into:
- White fish (like cod, haddock, coley, hoki, sole, pollack and plaice)
- Oily fish (like salmon, trout, mackerel, sardines and fresh tuna)
- Shellfish and other seafood (like prawns, crab, lobster, mussels and cockles)

Each kind is super-healthy in a different way.

White fish – the slimmer's friend:
- Extremely low in calories
- Extremely low in fat (especially the harmful saturated fat)

Oily fish – good for your heart:
- Rich in heart- and brain-healthy oils called omega-3 essential fatty acids
- Rich in vitamin A and vitamin E, and a good source of vitamin D

Shellfish – good for minerals:
- Crab and mussels are reasonable sources of omega-3s
- Shellfish are good sources of the minerals selenium, zinc, iodine and copper

Get fish on the menu

We should eat fish at least twice a week, and oily fish at least once. And more is better, provided that you follow certain safety recommendations.

Some oily fish can contain low levels of pollutants, which can build up in the body over time. Because of this, pregnant women and

children should avoid swordfish, marlin and shark, and the rest of us shouldn't eat these more than once a week, as they tend to have the highest levels of chemicals.

Many people wrongly believe that fish is tricky and time-consuming to cook, but it's actually quick, simple and delicious. What could be simpler than grilling or baking a piece of fresh salmon and serving it on a bed of salad leaves with steamed green beans and baby new potatoes? Or opening a tin of sardines, brushing them with Worcester sauce, placing them on crisp slices of wholemeal toast and grilling them until piping hot for a quick snack or simple lunch?

EGGS

Eggs have had a lot of bad press – people worried that they weren't safe, were high in fat and cholesterol, and bad for your heart. But provided you buy 'Lion-marked' eggs they're now perfectly safe – the only people who have to be careful are pregnant women and people with weakened immune systems, who should make sure their eggs are well cooked.

Eggs are:
- Surprisingly low in calories – a medium egg contains 76 calories, less than most sweet biscuits, and far more filling and nutritious
- A good source of protein, in a form that's easy for the body to absorb
- Lower in fat than meat and chicken, and most of the fat they do contain is the healthy mono-unsaturated kind
- Rich in vitamins A, D and E and the B-vitamins
- A good source of phosphorus, needed for healthy bones and teeth, and iodine, for making thyroid hormone
- A source of the immune-boosting minerals zinc and selenium

DAIRY FOODS

Dairy products – milk, yoghurt, fromage frais and cheese – are highly nutritious. After all, they're all based on milk, which is designed to be a complete food for a growing animal.

If you don't have problems digesting cow's milk, it's a good idea to eat or drink three servings of dairy food a day.

> ### WATCH THE FAT
> Some dairy foods are high in fat, so choose low-fat versions wherever possible. Choose:
> - Skimmed or semi-skimmed rather than full-cream milk
> - Low-fat rather than full-fat, Greek or Greek-style yoghurt or fromage frais
> - Cottage cheese or low-fat soft cheese, rather than full-fat soft cheese or cheese spreads
> - Cream? Who needs it when you can have delicious lower-fat alternatives like low-fat yoghurt, fromage frais or Quark (a low-fat soft cheese)

Milk

Which milk to choose? Generally the answer will be semi-skimmed or skimmed, depending on what's most important to you.
- Skimmed milk is lower in fat and calories than semi-skimmed milk
- Semi-skimmed milk is higher in the fat-soluble vitamins (vitamins A, D and E) than skimmed milk

- Whole milk (full fat)   4% fat
- Semi-skimmed milk   1.7% fat
- Skimmed milk   0.2% fat

One portion could be:
- A glass (200ml) of semi-skimmed or skimmed milk
- A small pot (150g) of low-fat yoghurt or fromage frais
- A matchbox-sized (30g) piece of cheese

So, while semi-skimmed milk is slightly more nutritious, skimmed milk is probably a better choice if you're trying to lose weight.

UHT (Ultra Heat Treated) milk doesn't have to be kept in the fridge until you open the carton, then it should be treated as fresh milk. It's a handy addition to your store cupboard – you'll never have an excuse to be out of milk!

Most of the milk drunk in the UK is semi-skimmed cow's milk, but you can also buy goat, ewe or even buffalo milk. These are generally higher in fat, and have different tastes. Some people who are sensitive to the proteins in cow's milk find they can drink milk from these other animals. However, if you're sensitive to the lactose, or 'milk sugar', in milk (lactose intolerance), you'll probably have problems with all animal milks, and be best drinking soya, rice or oat milk instead. Look for those that are fortified with vitamins and minerals, especially calcium. They all taste different, and some are slightly sweetened with fruit juice, so experiment until you find your favourite.

Tip: Some non-dairy milks don't respond well to heating, and may curdle or split when you add them to hot liquids such as tea or coffee.

Yoghurt

Yoghurt can be made from skimmed, semi-skimmed or whole milk – the kind of milk determines the fat content of the finished product.

Bio-yoghurt is made using special strains of bacteria called bifidobacteria or Lactobacillus acidophilus. It has a milder taste than other yoghurts, and might be beneficial to digestive health. However, although yoghurt is a healthy food, it's unlikely that just eating one or two bio-yoghurts a day will have much impact on your digestive health. If your digestion is troubling you, turn to page 212 for advice on a gut-friendly diet.

Many types of yoghurts contain several teaspoons of sugar – check the labelling and go for those with the lowest amount. And while 'diet' yoghurts may be low in calories and sugar, they'll still contain artificial sweeteners. Low-fat natural yoghurt is the healthiest kind – you can always add your own fruit, either chopped or pureed.

Cheese

Cheese is basically concentrated milk – it takes about 10 litres of milk to make 1kg of cheese. This makes cheese a brilliant source of protein, calcium and vitamins A and D. A small matchbox-sized piece of Cheddar (30g) contains about 30 per cent of the recommended daily calcium intake for an adult.

However, on the down side, the fat is concentrated too – much more concentrated than in milk. While Channel Island milk (the highest-fat milk of all) has a fat content of 5 per cent, Cheddar cheese is 35 per cent fat – and most of this fat is the harmful saturated kind. Also, most cheeses are high in salt.

So, must you avoid cheese if you're concerned about your health or watching your weight? Of course not – moderation is the key. Enjoy the taste and nutritional benefits of cheese, but choose carefully to minimise the fat.

As a rule, soft cheeses are lower in fat than hard cheeses. However, some cream cheeses, including mascarpone, can be higher in fat than hard cheeses like Cheddar, with up to 75 per cent fat. If you like their creamy taste and spreadability, look for low-fat soft cheese instead. Avoid 'cheese spreads' – they're generally full of artificial additives.

'Moderation is the key. Enjoy the taste and nutritional benefits of cheese, but choose carefully to minimise the fat'

COTTAGE CHEESE

Cottage cheese is practically 'guilt-free' cheese – it's low in fat and relatively low in salt.

Regular cottage cheese is only 4 per cent fat, and low-fat cottage cheese contains just 1.5 per cent. And 100g of plain cottage cheese contains 0.75g of salt – that's about an eighth of your recommended daily salt allowance.

Low-fat cottage cheese is a useful, healthy source of protein. It's ideal for quick and tasty salads, and as a dip with crudités. Well-drained cottage cheese also makes a good filling for pitta bread pockets and tortilla wraps – just add some fresh salad vegetables or roasted peppers and mushrooms.

For variety, add these to your cottage cheese:
- A couple of tablespoons of cooked diced chicken
- A slice of chopped lean cooked ham or turkey (on the bone, not re-formed)
- Two tablespoons of cooked chopped prawns (defrosted if frozen)
- A tablespoon of chopped pineapple (you can use tinned in juice, drain first)
- Two tablespoons of finely chopped red and/or green pepper

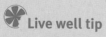

Live well tip

Get into the bean scene – try to include at least four servings of pulses in your diet each week.

Pulses

It's a shame pulses (beans and lentils) have such an unglamorous reputation. These vegetable proteins are veritable superfoods, which can lower your blood pressure and cholesterol level, help stop you putting on weight, balance your blood-sugar levels and decrease your risk of heart disease and cancer.

Pulses are high in fibre, with all the benefits that brings (see page 39).

They're also good sources of:

- B-vitamins
- Iron
- Folic acid
- Potassium
- Magnesium
- Phytochemicals (beneficial plant chemicals)

Now that many different kinds of pulses are conveniently available in tins, we can't make the excuse of them being time-consuming to prepare. With just a few tins of beans and lentils in your store cupboard, you have the makings of a wide variety of quick, delicious and nutritious meals.

When buying tinned beans always check the salt content – some can be unacceptably high, so look for 'low sodium' or 'no added salt' on the labels.

Tofu and other soya products

Soya beans provide the highest-quality protein of all the pulses. They also appear to reduce your risk of cardiovascular disease (heart attacks and stroke) thanks to phytochemicals (plant chemicals) called isoflavones.

'When buying tinned beans always check the salt content'

Don't forget
fresh beans and peas, they're all members of the same family – runner beans, French beans, Kenya beans, peas, mangetout and sugar-snaps.

Soya products aren't just for vegetarians – they're a good way of varying the protein in your diet, so try meat substitutes such as soya mince, soya chunks and soya burgers. Read the labels when buying processed foods – many are high in fat and salt. Remember that a soya-mince lasagne from the supermarket is still a processed ready-meal, and probably far less healthy than one you'd make yourself from 'plain' soya mince.

Tofu is bean curd, made from soya beans. It's high in protein, low in calories and fat, and, although (unlike other pulses) it's low in fibre, it's a great source of calcium. 'Plain' tofu tastes very bland, but you can buy it marinated, or soak it yourself in a tasty marinade – it absorbs flavours like a sponge!

Soya milk is also made from soya beans – it's undeniably different in taste to cow's milk, but don't let that put you off. Try different brands – they're all different. Look for one with added calcium (as soya milk is naturally much lower in this mineral than cow's milk).

NUTS AND SEEDS

Nuts and seeds may be small but they're perfectly formed, because they're packed full of nutrients. They are:

● Rich in protein
● High in fibre
● High in heart-healthy unsaturated fats
● Good sources of vitamins, especially B-vitamins, folic acid and vitamin E
● Good sources of minerals, especially potassium, magnesium, calcium, iron and zinc

Different nuts and seeds have different nutritional star qualities, so try to eat a variety.

Remember, though, nuts and seeds are also a high-fat food – even healthy unsaturated fats can pile on the calories, so don't be tempted to overindulge on nuts if you're watching your weight. We all know how moreish they are!

Buy your nuts and seeds 'plain', rather than salted. Eat them as they are, or dry roast them in the oven or a dry frying pan (watch them carefully to check they don't burn) to bring out the nutty taste. Add a sprinkling of cayenne pepper for a bit of extra kick.

Ideas:
● Eat a small handful of nuts as a snack, with some raisins or other dried fruit if you like some sweetness too – keep a small pot of them in your desk at work, or in the car
● Eat sunflower and pumpkin seeds as a snack
● Sprinkle seeds or chopped nuts on muesli or other breakfast cereals, or as a topping for yoghurt or frozen yoghurt
● Add seeds or chopped nuts to sweet or savoury crumble toppings

✽ **Live well tip**
Go nuts – Eat a tablespoonful of nuts or seeds every day.

Foods For Living And Doing

'Sugars are present in nature, for example the fructose, or fruit sugar, in fruit and the lactose, or milk sugar, in milk'

These are your energy foods, used to fuel every organ in the body.

CARBOHYDRATES

Carbohydrates (along with fats) are one of the body's two main fuel sources. They can be divided into two types:

- Sugars, or 'simple' carbohydrates
- Starches, or 'complex' carbohydrates

Sugars

Simple carbohydrates (sugars) are quick and easy for the body to break down into glucose, for energy. They supply a lot of energy, but it doesn't last long. When you eat a chocolate muffin, it gives you a rush of blood sugar, but soon your sugar levels fall, leaving you hungry again – and probably craving another muffin!

GOOD SUGARS?

When people talk about sugar, they generally mean refined table sugar, or sucrose. But sugars are present in nature, too, for example the fructose, or fruit sugar, in fruit and the lactose, or milk sugar, in milk.

These natural sugars are better for us than refined sugar. Fruit sugars don't cause such a rapid blood-sugar 'spike', because the fibre in the fruit means it takes longer for the body to break down and release the calories. And the sugars in fruit also come packaged with vitamins, minerals and health-giving phytochemicals (plant chemicals).

All this makes fruit an ideal way of satisfying a sweet tooth.

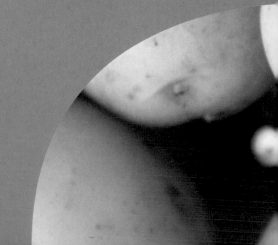

Starches

The body needs glucose for fuel, but it prefers not to get it in neat sugar form. What you really need is a steady supply of energy, rather than a big burst that doesn't last. You want 'slow release' fuel. This means foods that take longer to break down, and are therefore slower to release their energy.

Complex carbohydrates are broken down slowly, so they provide a slow rise in blood sugar, which lasts for longer, rather than a spike followed by a crash. In other words, complex carbs sustain you for longer. They keep you going between meals, allowing you to resist the mid-morning munchies.

Some starches are better than others. Refined (white) starches are quicker to digest, and release their energy almost as fast as sugars. Wholegrain starches, however, take longer to break down, and these produce a much more sustained rise in blood sugar – this is what you're after.

Think 'brown' and 'wholemeal' when choosing your starches or complex carbs. Choose wholemeal bread, wholemeal pasta, porridge oats, brown rice, bulghur wheat, millet, buckwheat and quinoa rather than the white versions of bread, rice and pasta.

Don't overcook potatoes
Potatoes boiled to powder are practically digested already, so it takes your digestive system no time at all to convert them to a blood-sugar rise.

What about potatoes?

Potatoes are high in starchy carbohydrates (as well as other nutrients, including the B-vitamins, folic acid, vitamin C and fibre), but they've gained a reputation for being 'fast-release carbs'.

But potatoes are too good for you to avoid! Turn them into 'slow-release fuel' with our tips:

● Eat the skins – the fibre makes them 'slower-release'. Try jacket potatoes, home-made baked oven chips or potato wedges with skins, or boiled new potatoes in their skins
● Add a tiny bit of olive oil – oil slows down the digestion time

HEALTHY FATS

If you thought we'd discourage fats in *You Are What You Eat – Live Well, Live Longer*, think again!

Yes, it's true that too much fat will make you pile on the pounds, with all the problems and health issues that brings. And some kinds of fats are bad for us, increasing our risk of diseases such as heart disease, cancer, stroke and even Alzheimer's.

But other fats have health benefits, and can reduce our chance of suffering from these conditions.

And we all need a certain amount of fat in our diets:
- For energy – fat from our diets, and fat stored in our body, can be broken down to provide fuel
- To protect our organs – although excess 'padding' isn't healthy, our vital organs, such as our kidneys and liver, need a thin layer of insulating fat to protect them
- To absorb and use certain vitamins, such as the fat-soluble vitamins A, D, E and K
- For healthy skin and hair – an overly low-fat diet can lead to dry hair and flaky skin
- To make essential hormones
- To build cell membranes
- For healthy brain function – our brains are composed of 60 per cent fat!

Unsaturated fats

As a general rule, the healthy fats are the kinds we refer to as oils – the ones that are liquid at room temperature.

'Healthy' fats can be divided into:
- Monounsaturated fats
- Polyunsaturated fats

Examples of monounsaturated fats include:
- Olive oil
- Canola oil
- Peanut oil
- Sesame oil
- Avocado oil

Examples of polyunsaturated fats include:
- Sunflower oil
- Safflower oil
- Corn oil
- Fish oils

The most important polyunsaturated fats are the omega-3 and omega-6 essential fatty acids – they're called essential because our bodies can't make them, so we have to get them from our diet.

OMEGA-3 ESSENTIAL FATTY ACIDS

These are brilliant for your heart, circulatory system and brain. They have been found to help:
- Keep your cholesterol levels under control
- Make your blood less 'sticky', and so less likely to produce life-threatening blood clots
- Treat and prevent inflammatory diseases like rheumatoid arthritis, lupus, Crohn's disease and ulcerative colitis
- Prevent and fight depression
- Prevent dementia

Think of omega-3s as 'fishy fats', because the best sources are oily fish, such as salmon, mackerel, pilchards, sardines and fresh tuna (the tuna-canning process removes most of the omega-3s).

Vegetarians can get much smaller amounts from flaxseeds (linseeds) or flaxseed oil. You can also buy vegetarian omega-3 supplements.

Live well tip
- Replace saturated fats with unsaturated fats
- Replace meat protein with vegetable protein (beans, lentils, etc.)
- Use a low-fat unsaturated-fat spread, in small quantities
- When you do fry foods, use olive oil

Omega-6 essential fatty acids

These beneficial oils have similar, though slightly lesser, heart-health effects to omega-3s. They may also reduce our risk of type-2 diabetes, and improve skin conditions such as eczema.

Omega-6s are found in nuts and seeds, as well as some vegetable oils – corn oil, sunflower oil and safflower oil.

WATER

Water isn't a fuel, but it's vital for survival. It's needed for every process in the body – including digesting and metabolising our food. It's also used for cooling the body, and removing waste products.

Our body weight is approximately two-thirds water, and losing only one or two per cent of this can leave us feeling distinctly below par and affect our energy levels and concentration.

This makes it vital to keep fluid levels topped up – aim to drink 1.5 to 2 litres of water every day. That's about eight glasses (children should drink eight small glasses).

WHAT TO DRINK

Your body is two-thirds water, not tea, coffee, cola, squash, wine or beer! Although all of these liquids will hydrate you, all of the list above (except for water) also act as diuretics, increasing the water you lose in your urine. This decreases their effectiveness in topping up your fluid levels.

Tea, coffee and cola are also stimulants, and cola and squash are high in sugar, sweeteners and other additives. Alcoholic drinks have their own long list of health implications (see page 100). That's not to say that from now on you should only ever drink water – tea and wine in particular have their own benefits, when drunk in moderation. But only count pure water towards your 1.5–2-litre target – that way, you'll be sure to stay optimally hydrated.

Milk

YAWYE verdict: **more of a snack than a drink**

Milk provides hydration (though obviously less than pure water) but its nutritional content makes it more of a mini-meal than just a drink. It's a good way of boosting protein and calcium intakes (especially for children), but watch out for the fat and calorie count if you're trying to lose weight. Stick to skimmed milk if this is an issue for you.

Fruit juice

YAWYE verdict: **whole fruit is better**

Fruit juice is full of vitamins, antioxidants and other phytochemicals, but also high in sugar. And because the fibre in the fruit has been stripped away, fruit juice causes a rapid 'spike' in blood sugar levels. The moral of the story? Fruit juice is good for you, but limit it to a glass per day – get the rest of your fruit in 'whole fruit' form.

Smoothies

YAWYE verdict: **a snack meal in a glass**
Smoothies are rich in vitamins and other fruity nutrients, and are higher in fibre than fruit juice, thanks to the fruit pulp. Smoothies with added milk or yoghurt are also a rich source of protein and calcium.

Fizzy drinks

YAWYE verdict: **avoid like the plague**

Full of sugar or artificial sweeteners, acid that erodes teeth, and generally also artificial colourings and flavourings. What more can we say?

Squash

YAWYE verdict: **dilute fruit juice instead**

Most squashes – even the high-juice ones – are high in sugar and/or artificial sweeteners, and sometimes colourings as well. It's better to make your own fruity drinks by diluting pure fruit juice.

> ‘Fruit juice is full of vitamins, but also high in sugar’

Juice drinks

YAWYE verdict: **don't be misled**

Don't get these confused with pure fruit juice – their actual juice content is generally rather low, and the rest is made up of water, sugar and (often) artificial sweeteners and colourings.

Flavoured water

YAWYE verdict: **what's the point?**

These manufactured drinks are generally just a blend of water and chemical additives. Why not just drink water?

Tea

YAWYE verdict: **healthy in moderation**

Our 'national drink' has a lot going for it – as well as being a welcome pick-me-up, tea contains health-giving plant chemicals called flavonoids which can help reduce our risk of disease, and may even slow down the ageing process. Tea can also reduce your levels of the stress hormone cortisol when you're under pressure. But tea also contains caffeine, and tannins, which hinder the uptake of nutrients from our diet. Because of this, avoid tea late at night if it keeps you awake, and drink it between meals rather than with them.

Herbal teas

YAWYE verdict: **a taste to acquire**

Herbal teas are caffeine-free, refreshing hot or cold, and many are reputed to have health benefits, particularly for relaxing. If you're new to herbal teas, try camomile or peppermint. You can also buy very pleasant herbal tea blends for various purposes, such as relaxation, uplifting, reviving, etc.

Green tea
YAWYE verdict: **worth a try**

Like black teas, green tea contains antioxidant polyphenols, but the plant chemicals found in green tea are slightly different. Population studies carried out in Asia, where the drink is very popular, suggest that five or more cups a day could reduce risks of heart disease and cancer.

Coffee
YAWYE verdict: **go carefully**

The most infamous source of the stimulant caffeine, coffee can make you feel good, and may decrease the risk of some neurological diseases such as Parkinson's. But it can also cause anxiety and jitteriness in susceptible people. If this sounds like you, try to find an alternative drink. For more on caffeine and coffee, see page 50.

When to drink
Don't wait until you're thirsty before having a drink of water – by the time you start feeling thirsty, you're already slightly dehydrated. Children and the elderly are particularly poor at judging thirst, so remind them to keep their fluid levels topped up.

It's better to drink little and often than huge quantities all at once. Don't drink large quantities during meals – a glass of water is fine, but too much can hinder your digestion.

'Coffee can make you feel good, but can also cause anxiety and jitteriness'

Foods For Performance And Protection

These nutrients:
- Kick-start the reactions that enable our bodies to function
- Protect us from illness
- Help us to recover from injuries
- Keep us in tiptop health

What are they?
- Vitamins
- Minerals
- Phytochemicals
- Fibre

Some of these nutrients are particularly important at different stages of our lives, and we'll be discussing them in more detail later in this book.

Vitamins

Vitamins are vital – that's what the first part of their name stands for. Vitamin molecules are tiny chemical enablers, setting off and regulating the reactions that digest our food and release its energy. They're also needed for good immunity, wound healing and to prevent vitamin-deficiency diseases.

Vitamins are only needed in tiny quantities, but, if you're not getting enough of them, you'll soon know about it. Even minor deficiencies can cause you to feel out of sorts, with symptoms such as tiredness or poor skin and hair. And, if the situation continues, your health will begin to deteriorate, and your susceptibility to disease will increase.

Different vitamins play different roles, and their huge range of functions and sources can appear mind-boggling. But don't worry – a healthy, balanced diet can supply all the vitamins most people need.

Vitamin	Function	Animal sources	Non-animal sources
Vitamin A	Healthy skin. Maintains the mucous membranes lining the mouth, eyelids, throat, digestive tract and vagina. Also essential for vision.	Liver, meat, oily fish, dairy products, eggs.	Green vegetables (spinach, cabbage, broccoli), yellow and orange fruit and vegetables (apricots, peaches, cantaloupe melon, carrots, sweet potatoes).
Vitamin B1, B2, B3, B5 and B6	Needed to release energy from food.	Meat, eggs, dairy products.	Unrefined cereals and grains, pulses, nuts, seeds, fortified breakfast cereals, green leafy vegetables such as watercress and spinach.
Folic acid (folate)	Helps the body to absorb nutrients effectively. Supports the immune system. Helps prevent a kind of anaemia.	Liver, eggs.	Green leafy vegetables, fortified breakfast cereals, pulses (beans and lentils), nuts, citrus fruit, apricots, broccoli, brown rice, wheat germ.
Vitamin B12	Needed for the production of red blood cells.	Red meat, fish, shellfish, eggs, dairy products.	Not found in vegan foods, but produced in small amounts by harmless bacteria in the gut.
Vitamin C	Supports the immune system. Required for wound healing. Boosts iron absorption from food.	None.	Fruit (especially kiwi fruit, blackcurrants, strawberries, citrus fruits), yellow and red peppers, tomatoes, Brussels sprouts.
Vitamin D	Absorption of calcium, needed for healthy bones and teeth.	Oily fish (e.g. salmon, sardines, mackerel), meat, eggs, dairy products.	A chemical reaction caused by the action of sunlight on the skin enables the body to make and store vitamin D. Vitamin D is also added to margarines and low-fat spreads, and fortified breakfast cereals.
Vitamin E	Needed for a healthy reproductive system, and supporting the immune system. Also important for nerves and muscles.	None.	Nuts and seeds and their oils, wholemeal bread, wheat germ, avocado, spinach, broccoli.
Vitamin K	Enables blood to clot injury. Needed for healthy bones.	Eggs, fish oils, dairy products.	Green leafy vegetables. Also produced in small amounts by bacteria in the gut.

MINERALS

Some minerals contribute to our bones and teeth – our bodies contain about 1.5kg of solid calcium, almost all of it in our skeleton and teeth. Others are less obvious – for example, potassium is involved in maintaining our blood's fluid composition and enabling our nerves to transmit signals.

Mineral	Function	Animal sources	Non-animal sources
Iron	Production of healthy red blood cells. Transport of oxygen around the body.	Liver, kidney, red meat, chicken, eggs.	Pulses (beans and lentils), green vegetables, dried fruit (especially apricots), fortified flour.
Calcium	Building and maintaining healthy bones and teeth. Nerve and muscle function.	Dairy products, tinned fish where the bones are eaten (e.g. sardines and salmon).	Tofu, sesame seeds, almonds, figs, kale and other green leafy vegetables, fortified flour.
Phosphorus	Forms part of our skeleton and teeth.	Meat, fish, eggs, dairy products.	Grains, seeds, pulses, fruit and vegetables.
Magnesium	Dealing with stress. Required for muscle function. Needed for healthy bones.	Meat, dairy products.	Green vegetables, nuts and seeds, pulses, wholegrains, dried fruits, mushrooms.
Potassium	Regulation of body fluids. Controlling blood pressure.	None.	Nuts (especially almonds and hazelnuts), sesame seeds, bananas, lentils, green leafy vegetables.
Zinc	Supporting the immune system and preventing infection. Sperm formation in men.	Oysters, meat, fish, shellfish, chicken, eggs, dairy products.	Seeds (especially pumpkin seeds), nuts, wholegrains, green leafy vegetables, pulses.
Selenium	Supporting the immune system.	Meat, offal, fish, seafood, eggs.	Brazil nuts, sesame seeds.

PHYTOCHEMICALS

As well as vitamins and minerals, plant foods (fruit, vegetables, grains and pulses) contain substances called phytochemicals – literally, 'plant chemicals'.

Phytochemicals make a huge contribution to good health and wellbeing. They include:

-  Quercetin from onions reduces inflammation and could help protect us from viruses
- Lycopene, found in tomatoes, reduces the risk of certain cancers
- Lutein and zeaxanthin, yellow pigments found in green vegetables, protect against age-related macular degeneration (an eye condition)
- Resveratrol, in red wine, is heart-healthy and may also help protect against some cancers
- Polyphenol flavonoids found in tea, cocoa and wine can also help make your blood less 'sticky', reducing the risk of dangerous clots

BETACAROTENE

The phytochemical betacarotene, from fruit and vegetables, can be converted in the body into vitamin A. This conversion is a safer way to get your vitamin A than eating large quantities of vitamin A-rich foods such as liver, or vitamin supplements (which contain 'pre-formed' vitamin A). Pre-formed vitamin A can accumulate in the body to harmful levels, but the body can't store and accumulate betacarotene. It's only converted as you need it, so you can't overdose. The worst that could happen to you if you ate too much betacarotene-rich foods, such as carrots, is that your skin could turn an orangey colour! And this hue would soon disappear as your diet returned to normal.

FIBRE

Fibre isn't even a nutrient, so why all the fuss about it?

Fibre, which used to be called 'roughage', has a bit of an embarrassing reputation, gaining an unfortunate connection in many people's minds with bowels and wind! But fibre is fabulously healthy. It can:

- Improve digestion, helping to prevent unpleasant conditions like diarrhoea, constipation and irritable bowel syndrome (IBS)
- Lower your levels of harmful cholesterol
- Reduce your risk of heart attacks and stroke
- Help control your blood-sugar levels
- Fill you up, helping you to maintain or lose weight

Most of us don't eat enough fibre – the recommended daily amount is 18g, and the average intake is only 12g (children need proportionally less, according to their size). But don't increase your fibre too suddenly – go slowly to give your gut time to adapt.

Fibre can be divided into:

- Insoluble fibre
- Soluble fibre

Insoluble fibre

This is the kind that most people associate with 'roughage' and healthy bowels. It absorbs water and provides 'bulk' in our diet, giving our digestive systems something to work on, and is great for preventing digestive problems.

Get it from whole grains, vegetables, fruit (including dried fruit), beans and lentils.

Soluble fibre

This is a 'gluey' kind of fibre that dissolves in water. It soaks up cholesterol in your blood like a sponge, reducing your risk of heart attacks and stroke.

Get it from oats, beans and lentils, and fruit (especially apples and strawberries).

FANTASTIC FRUIT AND VEGETABLES

Fruit and vegetables are the ultimate body protection and performance foods. If you want to live a long and healthy life, upping your fruit and vegetable intake could be one of the best changes you make to your diet.

They're rich in:
- Vitamins – they're particularly good for vitamin C and folic acid
- Minerals – many are a great source of potassium
- Other phytochemicals, such as the antioxidants that defend our bodies' cells from damage
- Natural sugars
- Water
- Fibre

So what, you may think, but what's in it for me?

 Live well tip
Get peel appeal – don't peel your vegetables and fruit, as most of the fibre (and much of the vitamin and mineral content) is found in and just below the skin. Wash your food well, and buy organic where possible.

Eating plenty of fruit and vegetables has been shown to:

- Reduce cancer risk
- Reduce heart disease and stroke risk
- Reduce cataracts risk
- Reduce Alzheimer's risk
- Reduce type-2 diabetes risk
- Help prevent birth defects
- Help keep your digestive system working smoothly
- Help you to maintain a healthy weight
- Help you to lose weight
- Improve your lung function
- Possibly slow down skin ageing

EAT 5-A-DAY

Eating five portions of fruit and vegetables a day may seem daunting, but if you spread them out throughout the day it's simple. Ideally we should all be aiming for seven to nine portions, but many people still have a long way to go to reach even five. The average intake in the UK is two or three portions (and women do better than men).

All it takes to reach your 5-a-day is a banana and a glass of pure fruit juice at breakfast time, a salad at lunch or a medium tomato sliced in your sandwich, an apple in the afternoon, and some vegetables with your supper. It is all a question of establishing a habit so it becomes second nature.

'Fresh, frozen and canned vegetables and fruit all count towards your 5-a-day'

WHAT COUNTS TOWARDS 5-A-DAY?
- A portion of cooked or raw fruit and vegetables
- A bowl of vegetable soup
- A serving of salad vegetables
- A glass of pure fruit or vegetable juice (only count once a day)
- A portion of cooked pulses (chickpeas, lentils, beans)
- A tablespoonful of dried fruit (only count once a day)

Fresh, frozen and canned vegetables and fruit all count, but it is best to aim for at least half of your daily intake from fresh or frozen sources.

WHAT DOESN'T COUNT?
- Potatoes (they're classed as a starchy food)
- Jam (not enough fruit to amount to a portion)
- The fruit in a cereal bar (once again not enough fruit)
- Squash, cordial and 'fruit juice' drinks (the fruit content is not high enough)

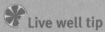

Live well tip

Spread smart – look for a fat that's low in saturates and high in monounsaturates. Olive spreads are healthier as a rule than sunflower spreads. Try to avoid spreads containing hydrogenated or partially hydrogenated vegetable oils.

Nutritional Bugbears

We live in a fast-food culture, surrounded by opportunities to fill our faces with fatty, sugary and salty junk food, and fizzy drinks loaded with sugar and chemicals. It's cheap, it's available, but it's not good for us.

But it *is* possible to eat healthily in a world where junk food is everywhere. You simply need to know what to choose, and what to avoid. And have the willpower to do it.

You've already learned about the healthy foods to include – your low-fat proteins, wholegrains, healthy oils and fruit and vegetables.

But it's all too easy for nutritional bugbears to slip into our diets. They sneak into a huge range of manufactured products, and not just the obvious 'fast food' – many foods that look quite healthy on the face of it have one or more of these lurking nutritional nasties.

- Saturated fats
- Trans fats / partially hydrogenated oils
- Refined sugar
- Salt
- Additives
- Caffeine

SATURATED FATS

Not all fat is the same – while we need some fat in our diets, and unsaturated fats such as olive oil and fish oils have their own health benefits, other kinds of fats are quite the opposite.

The most common 'unhealthy fats' are saturated fats, which contribute to atherosclerosis, or clogged arteries.
A diet high in saturated fats increases your risk of:

- Heart disease
- Stroke
- Certain cancers
- Alzheimer's

And because all fats are high in calories, they can cause us to put on weight, increasing our risk of a whole range of other diseases, such as diabetes and arthritis, as well as further increasing our risk of the conditions above.

Saturated fats are solid at room temperature. But not all of them are as obvious as a block of butter or lard. Much of the saturated fat we eat is 'hidden' in animal products, like meat, poultry and dairy. All of these are good, nutritious foods in moderation. It simply makes it all the more important to trim the fat from meat, and choose low-fat versions of dairy products.

There are only a few saturated fats produced from plant foods – the main examples are palm oil (or palm nut oil), coconut oil and cocoa butter (used in chocolate). However, coconut oil and cocoa butter are believed to have some health benefits that partially cancel out the effects of them being saturated fats. But that's not to say you should overindulge in chocolate or rich curries and Thai dishes!

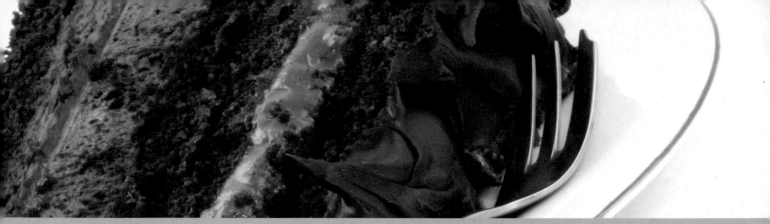

'It doesn't take much trans fat to have an adverse effect on your health'

TRANS FATS

Trans fats are even worse than saturated fats. They're just as calorific, have the same artery-clogging properties and could be even more carcinogenic (cancer-promoting) than saturated fats. Trans fats also seem to interfere with the use of healthy monounsaturated and polyunsaturated fats in our bodies, especially in our brains and nervous systems.

It doesn't take much trans fat to have an adverse effect on your health – getting just 3 per cent of our calories from trans fats (about 40 calories' worth) could be bad news. In fact, it's probably safe to say that the only truly safe trans fat intake is zero!

Almost all of the trans fats in our diets come from partially hydrogenated vegetable oils. These are an artificial invention of the food industry, used to replace healthier fats because they're cheaper and increase the shelf life of products.

These fake fats are in an alarming variety of processed foods: many ready-meals; packet mixes for cakes, desserts and sauces; ice cream, cakes, chocolate and confectionery; and 'instant' products such as soups and drinks.

Try to avoid products with 'partially hydrogenated vegetable oil', 'hydrogenated oil' or 'shortening' on the label. If it contains any of these, it contains trans fats. Remember that ingredients highest on the list make up most of the product.

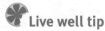

Live well tip

Keep it simple – It's really not that difficult to avoid additives – just steer away from processed foods, and make as many of your meals as you can yourself.

REFINED SUGAR

Refined sugar is a powerful energy source, but it can play havoc with your blood sugar levels.

It's also high in calories – only alcohol and fat are higher. And, what's more, many sugary foods are high in fat (think of cakes, pastries, biscuits and chocolate), which is a double-whammy to your waistline!

Sugary foods are also often 'empty calories', containing very few nutrients. For example, think of the spoonful of white sugar you might add to your tea or coffee. Aside from calories, that spoonful's nutritional content is a big, fat zero.

And although biscuits, pastries, cakes and chocolate contain other ingredients apart from sugar (so they're not so 'empty' as pure sugar and sweets) they're often high in saturated fat and additives, which are definitely not the kind of thing you want to be eating.

That's not to say that biscuits and the like are banned from a healthy diet – you just have to be sensible. Be aware that they're not so good for you, and save them for occasional treats. And try to make your own, rather than buying them – then you'll be in control of the ingredients.

'Eating too much salt can raise your blood pressure and increase your risk of heart disease and stroke'

SALT

Eating too much salt can raise your blood pressure and increase your risk of heart disease and stroke.

Just by cutting down on salt you can make one of the biggest positive changes to your health. If your blood pressure is high to start with, you can reduce it in just a few weeks, simply by making a few changes to your diet. Whatever your age and your blood pressure, reducing salt will lower that pressure.

Most of us eat too much salt – the recommended daily maximum is 6g per day, but the average intake for women is 8.1g and 11g for men. Most of that salt is 'hidden' – a shocking 75 per cent of the salt we eat comes from manufactured foods, rather than the salt we add ourselves.

People have grown used to the taste of salty food, so anything else tastes bland, but it's not so difficult to wean yourself off salty foods.
● Cut down on obviously salty foods such as crisps, bacon and foods packed in brine, such as olives
● Switch to low-salt versions of foods like ketchup and tins of beans and spaghetti
● When buying tinned vegetables, look for those canned in water (rather than brine)
● If you use stock cubes or bouillon powder, look for a brand that's low in salt (and free from hydrogenated vegetable oil)
● Cut down the amount of salt you add when cooking
● Use herbs and spices to season your cooking, instead of salt
● Don't add salt at the table, or at least taste your food first – it probably won't need it

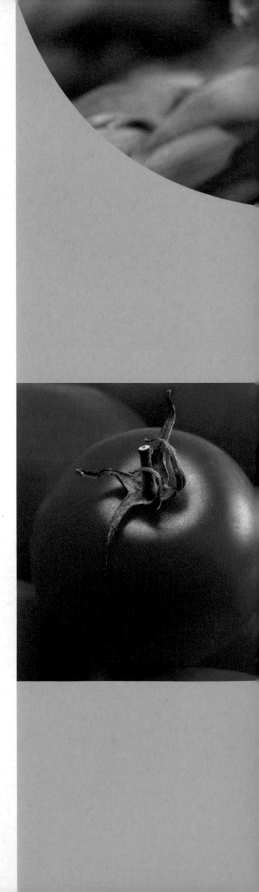

ADDITIVES

To give manufactured products the desired taste, appearance and
consistency, and to improve their shelf life, they often contain
artificial additives.

These may include:

- Colours
- Emulsifiers, stabilisers, gelling agents and thickeners
- Flavourings
- Preservatives
- Sweeteners

Additives as such aren't necessarily 'bad' – some 'natural'
substances, such as vitamin C, are added to some foods as a
preservative. And preservatives are responsible for preventing
bacteria and fungi from growing in our food.

All additives have been tested for safety, but many people are
concerned that the safety bar isn't set high enough. And many
additives seem unnecessary – the lurid colours added to sweets and
many children's products, for example. And a lot of products contain
artificial sweeteners, colourings and flavourings, where natural

alternatives could have been used instead. It's much healthier to buy a yoghurt flavoured and coloured with real strawberries, and sweetened with a tiny bit of sugar, than to eat one that's never been near a strawberry, and relies on chemicals instead.

Some people – particularly children – have bad reactions to additives. They may come up in a rash, or develop wheeziness or an upset stomach. Alternatively, additives may affect their mood or behaviour.

So, it makes sense to avoid products containing huge lists of artificial additives and E-numbers. And if there are any particular additives that you have found are a problem for you, always check the packaging before buying food.

EATING ORGANIC

If you're concerned about chemicals in your food, try to buy organic – look for the Soil Association symbol.

Organic farmers can only use four out of the hundreds of available pesticides (and as a last resort), and they don't use veterinary medicines on animals as a preventative measure – only when animals are actually ill. You won't find any genetically modified (GM) ingredients, hydrogenated fats, the artificial sweetener aspartame or monosodium glutamate in organic foods, and the levels or other additives are minimised.

CAFFEINE

Caffeine is the world's most popular 'drug' – many of us can't get going in the morning without a cup of coffee!

Caffeine undoubtedly gives us a buzz – it's a stimulant that perks us up and makes us more alert. It can also boost our exercise performance, and could reduce the risk of some neurological diseases.

But there's a darker side to caffeine – it can cause:

- Headaches
- Migraines
- Heart palpitations
- Sleep problems
- Problems in pregnancy
- Anxiety
- Shakiness

It also reduces the amount of iron we absorb from food, and increases the amount of calcium lost from the body.

You should cut down your caffeine intake if you're consuming more than four cups of coffee's worth of caffeine a day, if you appear to be very sensitive to its effects, or you suspect it's causing unpleasant symptoms such as anxiety, headaches or palpitations.

Don't worry about the occasional cup of coffee. But if you appear to be particularly sensitive to its effects, or you're drinking a lot of it, consider cutting down and replacing it with decaffeinated substitutes such as decaffeinated coffee, coffee substitutes, decaffeinated tea or herbal teas.

CAFFEINE – NOT JUST IN COFFEE

Food or drink	Caffeine content
Single espresso, Americano, etc.	130mg
Cup of filter coffee	100mg
Mug of instant coffee	100mg
Can of energy drink	Up to 80mg
Cup of instant coffee	75mg
Cup of tea	50mg
Dark chocolate bar	50mg
Can of cola	up to 40mg
Milk chocolate bar	25mg
Cup of hot chocolate	5mg
Cup of decaffeinated coffee	3mg
Cold cures / painkillers	Varies – check label

Pregnant women shouldn't consume more than 300mg of caffeine per day – high intakes can increase the risk of low birth weight or miscarriage.

'You should cut down your caffeine intake if you're consuming more than four cups of coffee's worth of caffeine a day'

Life Stage 1

you are™
what
you eat

A Healthy Start In Life

Eating a healthy diet from a young age gives you the very best start in life, building a healthy body and minimising the risk of chronic diseases later in life. Feeding children a healthy diet, encouraging a taste for 'proper' food and teaching them about good nutrition is one of the greatest gifts you can give your little ones.

YOUNG CHILDREN: 5–6 YEARS

Young children are growing rapidly, and their need for energy, protein for body building, and all the healthy fats, vitamins, minerals and phytochemicals they require for development, is extremely high.

But their tummies are small, and their attention spans short, so it's sometimes a struggle to get all the nutrients they need inside them. Small children can't eat a lot at one sitting, so they need small, tempting and highly nutritious meals.

We need to make sure they're not filling up on junk food – things like sweets, biscuits, crisps, cakes and fizzy drinks. Not only do they push out the healthy food children need, they also encourage a taste for fatty, salty and (especially) sugary foods, just at a time when children are particularly receptive to new tastes.

You don't want them to develop the preferences that will give them problems – making them overweight and harming their health – when they grow up. Good eating (and exercise) habits lead to better health that lasts a lifetime.

HAVE A TASTE

Introduce a variety of new and exciting foods you would like your children to eat, so that seeing new items on the table becomes commonplace. But don't mention the 'H' word. As young as this the merest hint that a food is 'healthy' can make them realise that this is somewhere they can exert a little of their growing independence by refusing to do something they know must be important to you. Concentrate instead on stressing that the new food tastes delicious and will give them plenty of energy for playing.

Don't be surprised if they say they don't like a new food the first time it appears. Research has shown that foods may have to be offered as many as eight times before children accept them. And there will probably be some foods that they simply won't like – ever.

HOW MUCH FUEL DO THEY NEED?

Small children can burn up an amazing amount of calories for their size, and when you're feeding a little one you generally don't have to use the same kind of caution that's advisable for older children and adults where fat is concerned.

Don't get overanxious about the fat in young children's diets, unless they have a weight problem. And certainly don't get hung up about calories! Yes, childhood obesity is a serious and growing problem, but young children, so long as they're as active as this age group should be, generally burn up all the calories they eat.

Instead you should concentrate on the kind of fats they eat – give them fish and foods containing healthy vegetable oils, rather than fatty meats, burgers, sausages, chips, and processed foods containing trans fats.

WHAT KIND OF MILK?

Above the age of three, children don't really need the fat and calories in full-fat milk. But skimmed milk is too low in calories, and in particular the fat-soluble vitamins A and D, so for this age group semi-skimmed milk is best.

HOW MUCH FIBRE?

Fibre is good for us, but it's filling. While this is great for adults and older children – it sustains us and helps us to resist unhealthy snacks between meals – too much fibre can fill small children up before they finish their meals, so they miss out on vital nutrients. Fibre also reduces the amount of certain minerals (especially iron) that children absorb from food.

You are really the best judge of your small child's appetite. If you are giving them a lot of wholegrain foods and pulses, and they say they feel full before they've finished, the fibre may be filling them too fast. Swap some of the 'brown' foods for 'white' versions such as 'ordinary' pasta, white bread or white rice, and see if this helps. You can always reintroduce the nuttier-tasting wholegrain versions later.

YOUNG CHILDREN AND WEIGHT

Although it's fortunately still fairly rare for young children to put on more weight than is good for them, the number of small children carrying too many pounds is rising. If this is the case for your child, you should consult your doctor for a specially devised weight-control plan for this age group, rather than putting your little one on a 'do it yourself' diet.

Breakfast – For Children And Everyone

Whether you're a scatterbrained schoolchild, a can't-be-bothered teenager, a stressed-out businessman or a harassed mum, breakfast is the meal most likely to fall by the wayside.

But your first meal of the day could well be the most important – breakfast kick-starts your metabolism in the morning.

Whether you eat breakfast, and what you have, affects what you eat for the rest of the day. Breakfast-eaters are more likely to eat healthily, while breakfast-missers are more prone to succumb to unhealthy snacks and overeating later.

If you miss breakfast, you're trying to function through low blood-sugar levels, fuzzy-headedness and poor concentration.

When children (particularly little ones) climb out of bed in the morning, they won't have eaten for ten to twelve hours. Their blood-sugar levels will have dropped overnight and if they don't eat breakfast they will dip even lower, producing physical symptoms like headaches, tiredness and dizziness.

Children who eat breakfast:
- Are better able to concentrate in lessons
- Tend to find problem-solving easier
- Have more stamina for playtime and PE lessons
- Are less likely to be 'troublesome' in class
- Are less likely to eat fatty or sugary snacks at break time

It has also been found that children who don't eat breakfast are unlikely to meet their daily requirements of some of the vitamins and minerals they need for growth and development.

A good breakfast should provide protein, slow-release wholegrain carbohydrate and preferably some fruit for vitamin C and other vitamins, minerals and phytochemicals.

Few of us have time to cook breakfasts on weekdays, but there are plenty of quick and simple cold alternatives, or items that can be cooked in advance and reheated, such as porridge. Then at the weekend you can ring the changes with reduced-sugar reduced-salt baked beans or scrambled egg on toast, or perhaps grilled mushrooms and tomatoes.

Some easy children's breakfasts:
- A bowl of no-added-sugar-or-salt muesli with semi-skimmed milk, topped with a portion of fresh or tinned fruit (in juice not syrup). A small glass of fresh orange, apple or grapefruit juice diluted with water
- A bowl of porridge made with half milk and half water, drizzled with a little honey or a teaspoon of sugar. A slice of toast, spread with a little spread and some low-sugar jam or fruit spread. A small glass of fresh orange, apple or grapefruit juice diluted with water
- Two slices of wholemeal toast with peanut butter or low-sugar jam. A piece of fruit and a small glass of semi-skimmed milk
- A chicken or lean ham sandwich (or toasted sandwich) with a piece of fruit and a small low-fat yoghurt. A small glass of fresh orange, apple or grapefruit juice diluted with water
- A small bagel spread with cottage cheese with pineapple. An orange and a small glass of semi-skimmed milk
- A fruit smoothie made with semi-skimmed milk and yoghurt. A slice of wholemeal toast spread with low-sugar jam

Live well tip
Bars aren't best – try to avoid cereal and breakfast bars for breakfast. They may seem a speedy option, but they're often high in sugar, fat and salt.

'Few of us have time to cook breakfasts on weekdays, but there are plenty of quick and simple cold alternatives'

- A bowl of wholegrain low-sugar cereal topped with fruit and a spoonful of natural yoghurt. A slice of wholemeal toast, spread with a little low-fat olive spread and some low-sugar jam or fruit spread. A small glass of fresh orange, apple or grapefruit juice diluted with water
- A toasted wholemeal English muffin topped with fresh berries, a tablespoon of natural yoghurt (and a drizzle of honey if you like). A small glass of milk

For adults, slightly increase the portions, or add an extra slice of toast, or fruit.

Delicious Breakfast Recipes

FRUITY BUN BREAKFAST
(Serves 2)

Health fact
Fresh fruit is an excellent source of immune-boosting phytochemicals and fibre, which is great for your heart and digestive system.

A selection of fresh fruit, washed and chopped – banana, kiwi fruit, seedless grapes, apple, pear, strawberries, nectarine, peach, blueberries
2 small cartons of natural low-fat Greek yoghurt
2 currant buns, split and lightly toasted
2 tsp runny honey

1. Arrange a selection of fruit in the centre of a plate, spoon on the yoghurt.
2. Cut the toasted bun into cubes and scatter over the yoghurt. Drizzle over the honey.

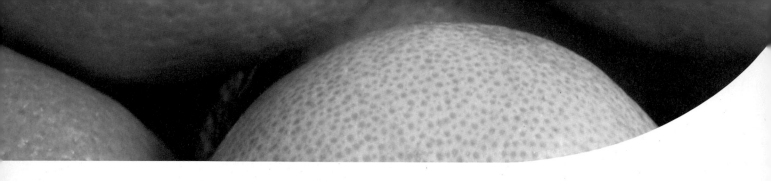

ORANGE AND WALNUT BREAKFAST SCONES
(Makes 6–8)

200g/8oz white self-raising flour
25g/1oz wholemeal self-raising flour
Pinch of salt
50g/2oz unsalted butter or low-fat olive oil spread, diced
Grated zest and juice of a small orange
115g/5oz walnuts, chopped
2 tsp caster sugar

1. Preheat the oven to 220C/Gas 8. Lightly oil a baking sheet.
2. Put the flour, salt and butter into a bowl and rub in the butter until the mixture resembles fine breadcrumbs (this stage can be done in a food processor and then the mixture transferred into a bowl).
3. Add the orange zest, the sugar and walnuts and stir into the mixture. Reserve 2 tablespoons of the juice and make the remainder up to 120ml/4fl oz with water in a small bowl. Add the juice and water to the dry mixture and mix to a firm dough. If the dough is too dry add a little more water.
4. Turn the dough out on to a floured surface and roll out to 2.5cm/1 inch thick. Cut out the scones using a round cutter. Re-roll the trimmings to make more scones.
5. Transfer the scones to the baking tray. Brush the tops with the reserved orange juice and bake for 15–20 minutes until the scones are well risen and golden. Transfer to a wire rack and cool.

These scones are delicious served spread with a pure fruit spread and a dessert spoonful of set natural yoghurt.

Health fact
These scones are low in unhealthy saturated fat, while the walnuts provide plenty of unsaturated fat, which is good for the heart.

PEAR AND BANANA SMOOTHIE
(Serves 2)

1 ripe pear, peeled, cored and quartered
1 ripe banana, peeled and sliced
5 tbsp low-fat natural yoghurt
150ml/1/4 pint skimmed milk

Place all of the ingredients in a blender and whiz until smooth. Divide between 2 glasses and serve at once.

TOMATO AND EGG MUFFINS
(Serves 4)

4 wholemeal English muffins
2 beefsteak tomatoes, halved
Ground black pepper
4 eggs
Low-fat olive spread

1. Cut the muffins in half and toast. Season the tomato halves with black pepper and grill until softened but not collapsed.
2. Pour boiling water into a frying pan to a depth of about 4cm. Keep the water just bubbling, and break an egg into a small bowl, then slide it into the simmering water. Repeat with the other eggs. Cook for 4 minutes, or until the whites of the eggs are set. Remove from the pan using a slotted spoon.
3. Lightly spread the grilled muffins with low-fat olive spread. Take four plates and place 2 toasted halves of muffin on each plate. Top one of the muffin halves on each plate with a tomato and the other with a poached egg.
4. Serve immediately.

STUFFED TOMATO BREAKFAST

(Serves 4)
You can make these the night before and store in the fridge, ready to bake in the morning.

4 large tomatoes
100g/4oz mushrooms, finely chopped
1 tsp fresh parsley, chopped
Ground black pepper
1 slice wholemeal bread, grated
1 tsp Worcestershire sauce
1 egg
4 slices wholemeal bread, toasted

1. Preheat the oven to 180C/Gas 4.
2. Cut a slice off the top of each tomato and scoop out the seeds using a teaspoon. Place the seeds into a bowl with the mushroom, parsley, ground black pepper, breadcrumbs, Worcestershire sauce and the egg. Mix well together. Fill the tomatoes with the stuffing and place on a baking tray. Bake in the oven for 20–25 minutes or until the tomatoes are tender.
3. Serve on a slice of wholemeal toast.

Top Nutrients For Young Children

Omega-3 essential fatty acids

The essential fatty acids make up an essential part of our body's cell membranes, especially in the brain and nervous system, so they're particularly important for young children, whose brains are developing at an incredible rate.

Some fascinating studies have shown that children suffering from behavioural and attention-deficit problems tend to be deficient in omega-3 EFAs, and that supplementing their intake can drastically improve their symptoms. Most children don't get enough omega-3s, and it's been suggested that increasing their omega-3 intake could make *any* youngster calmer and more focused.

It's thought that trans fats could interfere with the proper incorporation of omega-3 fats into the brain – all the more reason to keep processed foods (the main source of trans fats) to a minimum.

The best sources of omega-3s are the oily fish – salmon, mackerel, sardines and the like, though flaxseed oil provides lesser amounts. And these healthy fats are heart-healthy as well, yet another reason to encourage children to eat more of them.

However, the amounts of omega-3s used in the scientific studies that showed such remarkable improvements in conditions such as Attention Deficit Hyperactivity Disorder (ADHD) were high and would be very difficult to achieve through diet alone. If you think your child would benefit from omega-3 supplements, ask your doctor or a dietician or registered nutritionist to advise you on the correct dosage and form.

Vitamin A

This is vital for the continuing development of the brain and nervous system, as well as for immunity. Get it from lean meat, oily fish and green and yellow vegetables.

Zinc

Young children require a good supply of zinc, for immunity, and also for the conversion between the different omega-3s and omega-6s needed in the brain. Good zinc sources include meat, dairy products, nuts and seeds.

Vitamin C

Another immunity nutrient, important when children are starting school and coming into contact with all those other children – and their germs!

FIVE SUPERFOODS FOR YOUNG CHILDREN

- Carrots – full of betacarotene, a phytochemical that the body can also use to make vitamin A
- Apples – sweet and crunchy, with heart-healthy soluble fibre
- Salmon – full of omega-3s for healthy brain development
- Eggs – a brilliant source of protein and vitamins A and D
- Strawberries – great for vitamin C, and what child can resist them?

'Young children require a good supply of zinc, for immunity'

ADDITIVES

Food additives, especially artificial colourings, have been blamed for causing hyperactivity in children, and linked with problems such as ADHD.

The scientific jury is still out, but observational evidence from the families of hyperactive children certainly suggests that some additives cause behavioural problems in some children.

If you think additives could be affecting your child's behaviour, you need to do a bit of detective work, and narrow down the foods that appear to be triggers, until eventually you find out which one or more additives could be contributing to the problem.

To cut down on additives in general, try to make as much of your family's food from scratch as possible, and when you're shopping:

- Buy organic where possible – there are far stricter rules governing the additives allowed in organic ranges than for other foods
- Buy the best quality you can, because cheaper ranges tend to contain more additives
- Foods with long shelf lives generally contain additives to preserve them, so look for foods with shorter shelf lives, or frozen foods
- Avoid luridly coloured products – processed foods are often coloured just to make them appealing to children
- Check where the sweetness comes from – it's not just 'diet' products that contain artificial sweeteners
- If the label says 'no artificial colourings or preservatives' on the label, don't assume it's additive free. It could still contain artificial flavourings

HEALTHY TEETH

Children start to get their second set of teeth by the time they are around six years old and, as these permanent teeth should last a lifetime, it's essential they learn how to keep them strong and healthy. As well as good dental hygiene, what children (and adults) eat and drink – and when – plays a crucial role in keeping their teeth healthy.

A recent government survey found that 45 per cent of schoolchildren in Britain have dental decay by the time they are five years old and this rises to 58 per cent by the mid-teens.

Sugary foods and drinks are teeth's main dietary enemies, leading to decay and erosion of the enamel coating on the teeth. Each time we eat sugar the bacteria in plaque (the sticky coating on teeth) feed on the sugar and produce acid, which eats away at the teeth.

It's not only the amount of sugar that is eaten that matters – the frequency is even more important. Each time sugar is eaten, the bacteria in the plaque get to work, producing damaging acid. It takes twenty minutes for the acid conditions in the mouth to return to normal, so, if you eat sugar soon after, you start the whole vicious circle again, subjecting the teeth to another acid attack.

The sugars added to foods and drinks are the most damaging. The natural sugar (lactose) in milk isn't harmful, and as milk is rich in calcium and vitamin D (both important for healthy bones and teeth) milk is very tooth-friendly.

Other drinks, though, can be particularly damaging to teeth. Squash and fizzy drinks (including the low-calorie, sugar-free or diet versions) contribute to tooth erosion in their own right, as they are all acidic.

Tooth-healthy tips for children
● Minimise their intake of sugary foods and sweets – and reserve them for after meals
● Reduce the sugar and acidity of pure fruit juice by diluting it at least 50–50 with water and let them drink it though a straw, so the drink has less contact with their teeth
● After they've cleaned their teeth at bedtime, limit drinks to water
● Teeth should be brushed thoroughly but gently twice a day using a small blob of fluoride toothpaste
● Make friends with the dentist – children and adults both need six-monthly checkups

PROTECT YOUR GUMS

Don't neglect your gums! The bacteria that cause gum disease can escape into the bloodstream, where they trigger inflammation that can lead to damaged and clogged arteries, increasing your risk of heart disease and stroke.

The best way to help prevent gum disease is to floss regularly. As soon as they're old enough, get children into the flossing habit!

HARD CHEESE!
Fact: Research has found that a *small* piece of a hard cheese (such as Cheddar) after a meal, or to replace a sugary between-meal snack, seems to protect children's teeth against decay.

Juniors: 7–12 Years

Children need good nourishment to fulfil their potential, both in school and in everyday life. But just when children need to be eating really well, they start to rebel. Peer pressure and the influence of advertising begin to kick in, and the quality of many children's diets takes a nosedive.

Parents are the biggest influence on a child's eating preferences, so it's largely up to you to get them into the habit of eating healthily. Eating habits – good or bad – that are established in childhood can last a lifetime.

Children need:

- Enough protein for rapid growth – make sure it's high-quality, low-fat protein, not fatty processed foods
- Healthy monounsaturated fats to fuel activity and maintain a healthy heart and blood vessels
- Increasing amounts of wholegrain carbohydrates for energy, such as wholemeal bread, wholemeal pasta, brown rice, oats, bulghur wheat, millet and buckwheat
- Increasing amounts of iron, for muscle growth (especially in boys) and to produce red blood cells
- Calcium and vitamin D for growing bones and healthy teeth – aim for three portions of low-fat dairy foods each day
- Vitamin A for healthy skin and eyes
- Zinc for immunity
- Plus all the other vitamins, minerals and phytochemicals needed to keep a young body in tiptop condition

Nutrient focus – Vitamin A

Vitamin A is the 'skin and eyes' vitamin. And as well as keeping the skin that covers your *outside* healthy, it's also vital for your 'inside skin' – lining your mouth, the inside of your nose, your throat and the linings of your airways, the digestive tract and the lining of the womb and vagina.

It's also needed to produce a pigment in the retina of the eye, called rhodopsin, which makes it possible to see in low light levels.

On top of all this, vitamin A is a brilliant immune-boosting vitamin, helping your body produce infection-fighting cells. If you're deficient in vitamin A, your skin can become dry and flaky, and your resistance to illness can suffer.

Vitamin A is a fat-soluble vitamin that can accumulate to potentially harmful levels in the body if you eat too much, so it's important not to overdose on it. If you eat a normal, healthy balanced diet, you should be fine – problems generally only occur in people who regularly eat a lot of liver (the richest dietary source) or who take high-dose supplements.

The body can also convert the phytochemical (plant chemical) betacarotene into vitamin A and, because it's only converted at the rate you need it, eating betacarotene-rich foods is an ultra-safe way of getting your vitamin A. It's also the only way for vegans to obtain this vitamin – while pre-formed vitamin A comes from animal products such as meat, eggs, oily fish and dairy products, betacarotene comes from fruits and vegetables.

Betacarotene is an orange pigment, and the best sources of betacarotene tend to be the orange fruits and vegetables (though it's also found in green vegetables). Think of 'carrots for carotene' to help you remember – sweet potatoes, yellow and orange peppers, apricots and cantaloupe melons are excellent as well.

HOW MUCH SALT FOR CHILDREN?

The recommended maximum for children aged between seven and ten is 5g per day (equivalent to 2g sodium).

But boys actually eat an average of 6.1g of salt a day – that's nearly 25 per cent more than they should, and even more than the recommended maximum for a fully grown man.

Girls do better – they eat an average of 5.1g of salt per day, but this is still more than the recommendation, and they should be aiming for lower.

SCHOOL LUNCHTIMES

Most of us have two options when it comes to providing lunch for school-age children – packed lunches or school lunches. But a third option for a growing number of senior-school pupils is providing them with money to buy their own food, out of school, at lunchtime.

PACKED LUNCHES

Pros:

- You control what goes into the lunchbox
- You can provide a balanced meal
- Knowing what they had for lunch makes it simpler to organise the rest of the day's menus so they get a balanced diet
- Children may have more time to eat their meal as they don't have to queue in the school cafeteria

Cons:
- They can be more expensive to provide
- More time-consuming in terms of shopping and preparation
- Lunchboxes may not be stored in a cool place, resulting in a slight risk of 'food poisoning'
- Children may give away or 'trade' their healthy lunch items for less healthy ones

SCHOOL LUNCHES

Pros:
- Saves time for parents
- Children can get a hot meal in the day, a real plus in winter
- Nutritional standards of school meals have been improved and many junk foods removed

Cons:
- Parents have no control over the meal choices
- Children may still be able to choose a selection of 'snack foods' rather than a balanced meal
- Unless a swipe-card system is in operation they may spend their 'lunch' money on sweets and snacks on the way to school

BUYING LUNCH OUTSIDE SCHOOL

Available to some senior-school pupils, particularly in towns and cities, this is a popular option with teenagers. They see it as a chance to get out of school in the middle of the day. But a recent study in Scotland showed that for most children it was certainly not a healthy option. Despite being aware of the healthy-eating messages, left to forage for lunch they headed not for a healthy sandwich bar but to the nearest fast-food outlet or burger van parked near the school to buy burgers, pizza, pies, sausages, chips and more chips. Others made for the nearest supermarket or convenience store to stock up on items like family-sized bags of sweets, jam tarts, large packets of crisps and the almost obligatory litre bottle of fizzy drink.

'Children may give away or "trade" their healthy lunch items for less healthy ones'

If your child is allergic to a food, such as peanuts, you will obviously prepare packed lunches that are safe for them. But make sure the school knows about your child's allergy and enforces a 'no swapping' rule.

There is also the danger that children may decide to buy no lunch at all and save the money for things they consider more desirable, like magazines, CDs and computer games.

PACKED LUNCHES – KEEP IT INTERESTING

Let's concentrate on the one option where you can control what your child eats at lunchtimes.

Packed lunches needn't be boring – try to vary them, with different sandwich fillings, fruits, selections of veggie sticks and healthy treats. But don't fret if your child prefers to have the same items every day. It's more important that they actually eat their lunch, and you can always balance their diet with the food provided at other mealtimes and as snacks.

Make the portions appropriate to their age and appetite – too much in their lunchbox can be intimidating, particularly for young ones. Make sure any containers you use are spill-proof but that your child can open them easily.

Keep lunches for young children simple to eat, as they may find they're being given less time to eat their meal than they are used to at home. And they won't want to miss playtime with their friends!

Beware the 'children's lunchbox foods' now filling the supermarket shelves. Some of them are fine for busy mums, but read the labels – some contain high levels of sugar, salt or fat. And most of them, though convenient, are more expensive than similar items you could make or put together yourself.

What's in a healthy lunchbox?

Lunches should contain something from each of these food groups:
- Starch: wholemeal bread, rolls, pitta, bagels, wraps
- Protein: lean meat, fish, eggs, beans
- Fruit: any fruit that is easy to eat

- Dairy: cheese (in sticks or as part of a sandwich filling), low-fat yoghurt, fromage frais, a drink of semi-skimmed milk
- Drink: water or diluted fruit juice (not squash or fizzy drinks), semi-skimmed milk
- An extra: on most days, this could be a child-sized handful of dried fruit, or nuts (or a mixture), but occasionally slip in something like a piece of home-made fruit cake, a healthy home-made flapjack, banana cake, or a handful of baked potato crisps in a small container

Try to include some vegetables as part of the sandwich, or as an accompaniment.

As an alternative to a sandwich, older children may like:
- A flask of vegetable soup and a crusty roll
- A wholemeal pasta or brown-rice salad with chopped sweet pepper, halved cherry tomatoes and some cooked chicken, tinned salmon or tuna
- A slice of home-made quiche with a salad
- A slice of home-made (low-fat, low-salt) pizza and salad

KEEP THEM HYDRATED

Children who are dehydrated find it harder to concentrate in class, so give your child a trendy water bottle to take to school. Drinking water is now being promoted in schools as part of the Department of Health's National Healthy Schools Standard (NHSS) programme.

THE SNACK ATTACK

Adults often think of the snacks they eat as 'extras' or 'indulgences', but this isn't the right attitude. Snacks – provided they're healthy ones – are a useful way of sustaining us between meals and keeping our energy levels stable.

And where children are concerned snacks should be considered pit stops, vital to maintain their energy levels between more substantial meals. So it's important to choose snacks that add essential nutrients to their diets.

Live well tip

If your child isn't too keen on wholemeal bread, compromise by using one slice of white bread and one slice of wholemeal, or try one of the new breads which appear 'white' but have added fibre.

There's no need to try and remove every single unhealthy snack food from your child's diet. The very occasional handful of crisps, ice cream or chocolate bar will do them no harm. But, as with all less healthy options, the watchword is 'occasional'. Totally depriving children of foods they see their friends eating makes them feel left out, and the taboo item becomes even more desirable.

Smart snacking for children

- Plan ahead and stock up with healthy snacks – popping into the nearest convenience store or newsagent to buy a snack while you're out with your child often results in bad choices, particularly if they are pleading for a particular chocolate bar
- Let children choose some of their own snacks from healthy options
- Keep some healthy snacks like veggie sticks in the fridge so children can help themselves
- Try to combine two food groups when you are preparing snacks, such as a protein with a carbohydrate (see our Super Snack ideas below)
- Keep the snacks as far away from main meals as you can so you don't spoil their appetite

Super Snack ideas

- Two small wedges of cheese with a piece of fresh fruit
- A bowl of canned fruit and two oatcakes
- A peanut butter or fruit-spread sandwich
- A scoop of frozen yoghurt with tinned or sliced fresh fruit
- Raw vegetable sticks with a low-fat dip
- A small wedge of cheese, carrot sticks and two breadsticks
- A tablespoon of raisins and a small pot of plain fromage frais
- A handful of nuts and sultanas and a few low-fat pretzels
- Rice cakes topped with peanut butter
- A slice of fruit bread and a piece of fruit
- Half a bagel topped with a little cheese and popped under the grill
- A sliced hard-boiled egg with wholemeal bread and butter

LUNCHBOX TIP:

If you've got a breadmaker pushed away in the back of a cupboard, why not get it out and make your own bread for sandwiches? You'll know what goes into the bread and you can ring the changes by adding different ingredients, such as nuts, fruit and seeds. Children will love getting involved and helping to choose what to add to their bread.

BIG ISSUE – Immunity And Defence

In order to protect itself from disease and infection – from the common cold to cancer – your body needs strong defences. Without your immune system, every single germ you came across would lay you low, and you wouldn't last long, that's certain.

Your body also has defences, called antioxidant defences, against non-infectious diseases, that help prevent conditions such as heart disease and cancer.

Not surprisingly, the food you eat has an immense impact on your body's defences. If you supply it with all the nutrients your immune system needs to function properly, you'll have the best possible protection from bugs and germs, as well as from serious chronic diseases. But if you neglect your nutrition, eating fast food, fatty and sugary snacks, and ready-meals packed with additives, you'll also not only be clogging your body up with the things it doesn't want, you'll be starving your own defences of the very compounds they need to protect you from harm.

Eating for immunity

Are you one of those people who always feels below par, picking up every cold and snuffle that's going around? Do minor scrapes and cuts seem to take forever to heal? If so, your body's defences could be hungry for some good nutrition.

Your immune system determines whether or not you catch a 'bug' and, if you do, how long it takes you to shake it off. The immune system is very different to other body systems. The digestive system

'Not surprisingly, the food you eat has an immense impact on your body's defences'

and the circulatory system can be compared with a system of pipes and tubes. The immune system, however, is made up of several separate organs, including the thymus gland and the spleen, plus an army of free-roaming cells, which cruise around the body, looking for infectious trouble to deal with.

This 'army' is an amazing accomplishment of teamwork, with different kinds of cells working together to detect and destroy harmful germs.

In order to produce immune cells, and co-ordinate their complex activity, your body needs nurturing with good nutrition. When a country is stricken by famine, disease soon becomes a problem, and this is because malnutrition has a devastating impact on the effectiveness of the immune system.

On a much lesser scale, poor nutrition can weaken the immune system of 'well-fed' people in affluent countries like our own. Too few calories and too little protein (as in crash dieting) makes us vulnerable to illness. And, interestingly, so does too much fat.

Immune vitamins

High on the list of immune nutrients are the 'ACE' vitamins – vitamins A, C and E.

Vitamin A

This protective vitamin helps our skin maintain a strong barrier against the outside world, and all those germs. Vitamin A is also important for keeping the mucus membranes lining the nose, mouth, throat, digestive tract and lungs healthy, and these membranes help prevent germs that get into the lungs or digestive system from reaching the bloodstream.

You can get your vitamin A as 'pre-formed' vitamin A from animal sources, such as meat. But the body can also make vitamin A from betacarotene, which is found in orange and yellow fruit and vegetables.

Vitamin C

Vitamin C is probably the best-known vitamin, thanks largely to its reputation for stopping people from getting ill, and particularly from catching colds!

Unfortunately, it appears that vitamin C can't prevent the common cold, though taking it at the first sign of a sniffle can make the cold last for a shorter time.

However, vitamin C is excellent for boosting the immune system and promoting wound healing.

Don't let your fruit and vegetable intake slip in winter. Getting less of the immune nutrients during the colder months could be a major reason why people suffer more minor illnesses such as colds at this time of year.

Vitamin E

Vitamin E, as well as supporting the immune system, works alongside vitamin A to maintain the skin as a strong barrier against germs.

The B-vitamins

Notably vitamin B6, but also vitamins B1, B2, B12 and folic acid, are also important for a healthy immune system. They're involved in the production of antibodies – key players in the immune response.

Immune minerals

Zinc

This is probably the most important mineral for the immune system, and zinc defficiency could leave you vulnerable to infection. Zinc lozenges, taken according to the instructions, can help to treat sore throats, thanks to the mineral's antiviral action. But beware of overdoing the zinc – too much will actually suppress your immunity.

Selenium

Selenium is a trace element, needed only in minuscule amounts. But selenium is crucial for good health, particularly where the body's defences are concerned – various components of the immune system fail to work properly when we're deficient in selenium.

PROBIOTICS AND IMMUNITY
Probiotics, 'friendly bacteria' added to yoghurt drinks and also available in supplement form, could also boost your immune system. It appears that probiotics help to activate certain cells in the immune system, and studies have found that the beneficial bugs can cut the duration of the common cold by nearly a quarter.

THE IMMUNE SYSTEM HAS MANY ENEMIES – TRY TO AVOID:

- Stress
- Pollution
- Cigarette smoke
- Food contaminants such as pesticides
- Too little, or too much, exercise
- Obesity
- Crash dieting
- And, of course, poor nutrition

WHERE TO GET YOUR IMMUNE-BOOSTING NUTRIENTS

Nutrient	Source
Vitamin A	Meat (especially liver), eggs, dairy products, oily fish
B-vitamins	Meat, eggs, dairy products, wholegrains, pulses, nuts, seeds, fortified breakfast cereals, green leafy vegetables
Vitamin C	Kiwi fruit, blackcurrants, citrus fruit, strawberries, green vegetables (raw or lightly cooked)
Vitamin E	Nuts (especially almonds), seeds, and seed oils such as safflower and sunflower oil, eggs, avocados
Zinc	Lean meat (the richest source), seafood, dairy products, chick peas, pumpkin seeds and sunflower seeds, nuts such as cashew and pecan nuts
Selenium	Brazil nuts, fish (especially shellfish), kidney and liver

Recipes for a healthy immune system

The following recipes all contain nutrients which can help give a boost to the immune system.

MOROCCAN STYLE CHICKEN WITH SWEET POTATO
(Serves 4)

8 skinless chicken thighs, trimmed of as much fat as possible
1 tsp ground cumin
1/2 tsp hot chilli powder
Ground black pepper
2 tsp sunflower oil
2 medium onions, peeled and sliced
2 garlic cloves, peeled and crushed
2 medium sweet potatoes, peeled and cubed
400g/14oz can chopped tomatoes
3 tbsp fresh mint, chopped
3 tbsp fresh coriander, chopped
2 tsp organic stock powder
1 wide strip fresh lemon peel
50g/2oz sultanas

1. Preheat the oven to 180C/Gas 4.
2. Place the chicken thighs in a bowl, add the spices and toss. Season generously with ground black pepper.
3. Heat the oil in a large non-stick frying pan. Add the chicken and fry for 4–5 minutes until browned on all sides. Add the onions, garlic and sweet potatoes and cook for 3–4 minutes gently stirring regularly. Add the tomatoes, the mint, coriander, stock powder, lemon peel and sultanas. Bring to the boil. Transfer to a lidded oven-proof dish.
4. Bake in the oven for 1 hour. Serve with rice or fruity couscous and green beans or a salad.

Health fact
Chicken is low in fat and rich in protein – which is essential for growth and cell repair. Sweet potatoes are rich in betacarotene and help promote healthy skin and vision.

MEDITERRANEAN LAMB
(Serves 4)

4 lamb steaks, fat removed and cut into cubes
1 tbsp each chopped fresh thyme and rosemary (or 2 tsp dried mixed herbs)
Ground black pepper
1 tbsp extra virgin olive oil
1 medium onion, peeled and crushed
2 medium courgettes, cut into slices
1 red pepper, deseeded and diced
1 yellow pepper, deseeded and diced
400g/14oz new potatoes, cleaned and cut into slices
1 lamb stock cube
100ml/4fl oz just-boiled water
400g/14oz can chopped tomatoes
2 tbsp tomato puree
1 tbsp cornflour blended with 1 tbsp cold water to form a paste
Fresh basil sprigs to garnish (optional)

1. Heat the oven to 170C/gas 3.
2. Place the lamb in a bowl with the chopped or dried herbs and black pepper and toss thoroughly.
3. Heat the oil in a large non-stick saucepan and fry the lamb over a medium heat for 5 minutes until lightly browned. Add the onion and cook for a further 2 minutes then stir in the remaining fresh vegetables and cook for 5 minutes, stirring regularly.
4. Dissolve the stock cube in the water and add to the saucepan with the chopped tomatoes and tomato puree. Bring to the boil, add the blended cornflour and cook for 2 minutes until the liquid has thickened.
5. Transfer to a lidded oven-proof dish and bake for 1 1/4 − 1 1/2 hours until the meat is tender. Garnish with basil sprigs, if used.
6. Serve with fresh vegetables or a green salad.

Health fact
Lamb is a good source of protein and iron. Red and yellow peppers are a great source of vitamin C and betacarotene which the body converts to vitamin A – needed for healthy eyes, skin and immune system.

CHILLI TOMATO SOUP

(Serves 4)

1 tsp olive oil
1 medium carrot, peeled and finely sliced
1 onion, peeled and finely chopped
1 medium red chilli, deseeded and finely chopped
400g/14oz can chopped tomatoes
2 bay leaves
1 tsp caster sugar
600ml/24fl oz vegetable or chicken stock (made with a cube if you like)
Freshly ground black pepper
Chopped parsley to garnish (optional)

Health fact
Tomatoes are a good source of immune-boosting vitamin C, and carrots are great for betacarotene, which the body can convert into vitamin A.

1. Place the oil in a large saucepan and add the carrot, onion and chilli. Cook gently, stirring regularly for 5 minutes. Add the tomatoes, the bay leaves, sugar, stock and pepper. Cover the pan and simmer gently for 25 minutes.
2. Remove the bay leaves and allow the soup to cool for 10 minutes. Place in a blender and whiz until smooth (add a little more water if it is too thick). Return the soup to the pan and heat through – do not boil.
3. Pour into bowls and sprinkle with parsley if used. Serve with warmed crusty wholemeal bread.

MANGO CHILLI SALSA

(Serves 4)
A spicy accompaniment for barbecued and grilled chicken, meat and fish.

1 large ripe mango
1 small green chilli
1 small red onion
Zest of 1/2 lime
Juice of a lime

Health fact
Mangoes are an even richer source of vitamin C than oranges.

1. Peel and finely dice the mango and place in a bowl.
2. Remove the seeds from the chilli and slice the chilli very finely.
3. Peel and finely chop the onion.
4. Combine the mango, chilli, onion, lime juice and zest in a small bowl.
5. Transfer to a serving dish.
6. Cover and chill until ready to serve.

Health fact
Oranges are terrific for vitamin C, which helps support the immune system.

FRESH ORANGE DESSERT
(Serves 4)

4 large oranges
3 tbsp shelled pistachios (not roasted or salted), chopped
2 tsp runny honey (optional)

1. Remove the top and bottom of each orange with a sharp knife. Remove the remainder of the skin, making sure that you remove all of the pith. Cut the orange into circles. Arrange the circles on four plates and sprinkle over the chopped nuts. Drizzle with the honey if used.
2. Serve with low-fat fromage frais or yoghurt.

Health fact
Mangoes are an excellent source of antioxidants. They provide vitamin C, vitamin E and betacarotene, which the body converts into vitamin A.

RASPBERRY AND MANGO PANCAKES
(Serves 4)

4 good-quality ready-made pancakes, or make your own (see recipe on page 84)
2 mangoes, stoned and sliced
200g/8oz fresh raspberries
2 tsp honey (optional)

1. Place the pancakes flat on to 4 plates. Put the mango slices into a blender and whiz until smooth. Spoon the raspberries on to the pancakes and spoon over the mango sauce. Roll the pancakes and drizzle with the honey if used.
2. Serve with natural yoghurt or fromage frais.

PANCAKES
(Makes 8 pancakes)

150g/6oz plain flour
3 medium eggs, beaten
250ml/8fl oz semi-skimmed milk
1 tsp sugar
A little spray olive oil for frying

1. Sift the flour into a large bowl, then add the sugar. Make a well in the centre and add the eggs. Beat thoroughly and then gradually add the milk to make a thin smooth batter.
2. Lightly spray a non stick frying pan and add 3 tablespoons of the batter to the pan. Tilt the pan so that the batter completely covers the surface in a thin layer. Cook until bubbles appear all over the pancake, then turn to cook the other side. Keep the pancakes warm as you make them, until you have cooked as many as you need.

Pancakes can be frozen after they have been cooked and allowed to get cold. Before freezing interleave them with circles of baking parchment so you can take out as many as you need.

EXERCISE FOR IMMUNITY
A healthy amount of energy is a great boost to your immune system – half an hour of brisk walking, five days a week, is all it takes. Exercise is also a great stress buster, and stress puts a real dampener on your immunity.

Just don't overdo the exercise. 'Overtraining' actually suppresses the immune system. If your workouts are too long, too intense or you don't allow yourself enough rest in between, you'll leave yourself more vulnerable to illness.

> '**Oxidation is a process by which harmful molecules called free radicals damage our bodies' cells'**

Body defence and antioxidants

You've probably heard that foods rich in antioxidants are good for you. But how do they work? What are the 'oxidants' that these nutrients are 'anti'?

Oxidation is a process by which harmful molecules called free radicals damage our bodies' cells, and antioxidants protect us by mopping up the free radicals before they can cause this oxidative damage.

Oxidative damage is seriously bad news. It's at the root of many chronic diseases, such as heart disease, stroke and cancer. It even underlies the ageing process, so you can see why you ought to be getting as many antioxidants into your diet as possible.

Many of the immune-boosting nutrients also work as antioxidants, as do a whole host of the phytochemicals we introduced on page 38.

Eat plenty of these foods to boost your antioxidant intake:

Fruit and vegetables: The ultimate body-protecting foods, so eat as many as possible. Eat a variety, and as many different colours as you can, for maximum effect.

Two particularly potent groups of antioxidants are the carotenoids (including betacarotene) and anthocyanins – plant pigments that give fruit and vegetables their colourful hues. Here's where to find them:
- Carotenoids – carrots, sweet peppers, sweet potatoes, dark-green vegetables
- Anthocyanins – berries (especially blueberries), cherries, red grapes

Nuts and seeds: These are your best bet for the immune and antioxidant vitamin E. Eat them as a snack, as a topping for cereal or yoghurt, add them to baking, and sprinkle them on salads for extra crunch.

Wine and tea: Although we're not recommending that you overindulge in either, wine contains polyphenol compounds, and tea contains catechins, both of which are powerful antioxidants.

✳ **Live well tip**

Get in the pink – eat foods rich in the antioxidant lycopene, such as tomatoes, watermelon and pink grapefruit. They reduce your risk of cancer (especially prostate and breast cancer) and heart disease.

VITAMIN E

Vitamin E is a powerful antioxidant, and particularly effective in the lungs and the red blood cells. But as it works, mopping up harmful free radicals, it becomes damaged, and begins to act as an oxidant itself. This is where vitamin C comes in once more, 'recycling' the vitamin E so it can get back to work protecting the body's cells.

So you need plenty of vitamin E, and vitamin C to recycle it (and to act as an antioxidant in its own right). Get them from plant foods, like nuts, seeds, fruit and vegetables.

FOOD, NOT SUPPLEMENTS

Antioxidants eaten in food appear to be far more effective than supplements at protecting our health. Scientists have established that there are links between these nutrients and our health, but the vast majority of studies where people are given antioxidant tablets fail to produce the hoped-for benefits.

It seems there's something in antioxidant foods that just can't be replicated in pill form. And until that can be done, we should just enjoy as many healthy fruits, vegetables and other antioxidant-rich whole foods as we can.

Teenagers: 13–19 Years

Teenagers are growing and developing rapidly. Their energy and nutrient needs are higher than those of any other age group, so it's important to encourage them to eat a healthy balanced diet rather than satisfy their hunger with fast food and sticky cakes.

By the time they reach this age, young people have more choice than ever over their food and eat more of their meals away from home. But, even though you have less control over what your offspring eat, you need to remember this could be your last chance to help guide them on to the nutritional straight and narrow before they fly the nest.

What young people eat has an immediate impact on their health, affecting their energy levels and susceptibility to illness. And, probably more important to teenagers themselves, diet also affects their looks – whether they're slim or overweight, as well as the condition of their teeth, skin and hair. There is also increasing scientific evidence that nutrition in childhood and adolescence is linked to adult susceptibility to disease. It's a sad fact that in recent years the early signs of 'adult diseases' such as type-2 diabetes, high blood pressure and atherosclerosis ('furring' of the arteries) are being seen in teenagers and even younger children.

KEY NUTRIENTS FOR TEENAGERS

Omega-3 essential fatty acids

These are particularly important for adolescents, because of their involvement in brain function – omega-3s can help smooth the emotions and are essential for continuing brain development. Omega-3s also lower the level of 'bad' cholesterol in the blood, lowering the risk of heart disease and stroke later in life.

And both omega-3s and the omega-6s found in nuts and seeds are good for the skin – which is hopefully enough of an incentive for most teenagers to at least give them a try.

Iron

Iron requirements are particularly high during the teenage years. Girls' needs increase once their periods start, as they lose iron every month. And the iron requirements of teenage boys are even higher than for women, as adolescent boys are (hopefully) piling on muscle.

However, iron deficiency and anaemia are common problems in teenagers, and 20 per cent may be low in this mineral, causing symptoms such as fatigue, weakness and breathlessness during exercise. Anaemia can hamper teenagers' performance in school.

Many teenagers' diets are iron deficient – the average teenage iron intake is only 95.3 per cent of the recommended daily intake for boys, and 61.8 per cent for girls. Vegetarians may be more at risk from iron deficiency if they're not careful with their diets, and vegetarianism and veganism are common among teenagers – including up to 10 per cent of teenage girls.

Calcium

The rapid increase in bone mass during teenage years means that teenagers need just as much calcium as adults, and boys need even more. Twenty-five per cent of peak bone mass is acquired during adolescence, and an adequate intake of calcium reduces the later risk of osteoporosis, a particular risk in older women.

Folic acid

Once girls reach reproductive age (i.e. it's possible they could become pregnant), folic acid becomes particularly important. This is because folic acid helps prevent developmental defects in the foetus (see also pages 117 and 120).

Top iron sources: Liver, kidneys, lean red meat, other meat. Vegetarians can get iron from beans, nuts, dried fruit and green vegetables.

Vitamin A

Teenagers also need the immune-boosting antioxidant vitamin A, and once again the average teenager falls short – 15 per cent below the target. Vitamin A is especially important for vision and healthy skin, as well as reducing the risk of heart disease and cancer in later life.

Nutrient focus – Iron

Iron is used to make the haemoglobin molecule, which ferries oxygen around our bodies in our red blood cells. Not enough iron means too few red blood cells being made, which can leave us feeling weak, tired and breathless. If iron deficiency is allowed to continue, it can progress to anaemia.

Some people have extra iron needs:
- Toddlers – growing rapidly
- Teenage girls and women – start to lose iron when their periods start
- Teenage boys – gaining muscle
- Pregnant women – iron needed to build a baby
- Breast-feeding women – iron is passed on to the baby in the mother's milk

The main iron sources in the UK diet are flour and breakfast cereals (which are fortified with iron). Perhaps surprisingly, meat provides a smaller proportion of our iron. Other sources include potato, and vegetarian products such as tofu and other soya products.

Where we get our iron from is important. Iron from animal products is much easier for our bodies to use, whereas iron from non-meat sources is poorly absorbed by the body. Eating or drinking vitamin-C-rich foods (such as orange juice) with iron-containing foods helps iron uptake.

BODY IMAGE

TV and magazine images can lead to unhealthy desires for 'the perfect body', especially in young people. It is vital to encourage a sensible body image in teenagers, so emphasise the benefits and attractiveness of a healthy weight. A large proportion of teenage girls, and also some boys, are on or have been on dubious slimming diets. While shedding *excess* pounds is to be encouraged, unrealistic striving for a stick-thin physique can lead to eating disorders. Also, slimming diets often involve cutting out or seriously limiting food groups such as carbohydrates, meat and dairy products, which contain nutrients such as complex carbohydrates, fibre, a whole range of vitamins, plus iron, calcium, zinc and other minerals. Young people should be encouraged to ditch the faddy diets and instead go for sensible, healthy eating coupled with exercise.

SET A GOOD EXAMPLE

With younger children, parents are one of the principal role models for their food choices, but this changes when they reach adolescence. The influence of parents and other adults appears to wane, and teenagers become more vulnerable not only to peer pressure but also to the power of advertising – generally encouraging them to eat processed foods high in fat and sugar and low in vitamins and minerals. It's hard to prevent the influence of other teenagers and any negative comments you make on their friends' eating habits are almost guaranteed to make them even more appealing. A better way is to warn your teenagers about the slick ways of the advertising industry and the need to avoid being misled by claims. No teenager likes to think they're being taken in. But parents still need to set a good example. You can't slump in front of the TV with a takeaway fried chicken and chips and expect them to make healthy choices themselves.

Teenagers are smart. Don't preach, just give them the information, and make sure it isn't all negative. Show them that healthy eating doesn't equal boring, and that filling up with tasty fruit, vegetables and wholefoods will give them bags of energy and help them resist junk food and avoid piling on the pounds.

DON'T PREACH

Having struggled to gain some independence, adolescents like to think they are making their own decisions. In their eyes being told what to do is for children, so health messages for teenagers need to be non-patronising and appeal to the lifestyles they aspire to. Mentioning the link between adult diseases and diet is generally a turn-off, but pointing out how diet may affect their skin or their hair – things that matter to them here and now – is more likely to get them thinking.

Here are a few more 'here and now' strategies. Tell them that:

- They will be able to concentrate and do better at school if they eat breakfast
- They won't get hungry so quickly if they eat wholegrain carbohydrates rather than sugary food
- If they get enough iron in their diet they won't feel weak and tired, as iron is essential for building muscle – this will appeal to the sporty types
- Eating too much sugar could result in more visits to the dentist
- A bad diet can contribute to grotty skin
- Calories can lurk in unlikely places – make sure they know which foods are high in fat or sugar

THE UNIVERSITY CHALLENGE

Moving away from home to college or university (or to work) can be a traumatic time for teenagers, so it's not surprising that lack of cooking skills, time and money can lead many into bad eating habits. But if they leave home *knowing* how to eat healthily and how to knock up a few quick healthy meals from store-cupboard ingredients, not only will they be the envy of their new friends, you'll also know you have given them the best start you can.

Living in college accommodation

In their first year, many students live in halls of residence and, although campus dining halls and cafeterias are improving, there's no guarantee students will make the healthy choices. The chances are they'll find their favourites and stick to them week in and week out. Not only is this boring, but they'll also be likely to miss out on some vital nutrients.

But if a student makes their own packed lunch – a simple sandwich, a piece of fruit and a yoghurt – not only will they save the three or four pounds a day it would cost them to buy lunch in the cafeteria or at a local pub, they will be increasing the range of food they eat and also the nutrients.

Another danger spot for the nutritionally unwary is the banks of vending machines often provided to stave off student hunger pangs when the cafeteria is closed. These can be filled with all manner of highly processed foods loaded with sugar, fat and salt, such as sausage rolls, pies, instant noodle snacks, muffins, chocolate and crisps. Far better for students to stock up on fruit and vegetables, and eat raw healthy snacks from the local supermarket.

Live well tip
Set aside time for meals – it's all too easy, particularly in the first few hectic and bewildering weeks of studying, to exist on a succession of unhealthy snacks grabbed on the run.

'A danger spot for the nutritionally unwary is the banks of vending machines often provided to stave off student hunger pangs when the cafeteria is closed'

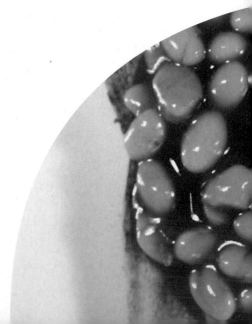

Shared accommodation

Students living in shared accommodation have the opportunities to eat healthily but, as anyone who has shared a kitchen knows, it's not always easy, particularly if everyone likes different things, yet wants to cook at the same time. You also need to know how to be selective with your shopping if you only have one shelf in a store cupboard and half a shelf in the fridge to keep your food.

Savvy shopping for students: eating healthily at college doesn't have to be expensive – here are a few ways to save:

- Shop for vegetables and fruit at street markets and greengrocers
- Buy fruit and vegetables when they're in season to get the best prices. You'll pay more for fruit that's flown halfway round the world
- Oriental and Asian supermarkets are great places for keenly priced beans, grains, pulses, and exciting spices
- Make friends with your butcher or fishmonger. He'll be happy to advise you on cheaper cuts and tell you how to cook them
- Compare the price of cheese bought loose from the deli counter with pre-packed cheese – it's often cheaper to buy it loose, and you can buy it in smaller quantities

- Buy strong cheeses rather than mild. You'll be able to use less and so you'll save (on fat and calories as well as cash)
- Stock up on items you regularly use when they're on special offer, such as tinned tomatoes and beans, and dried pasta
- If you've got freezer space, use it wisely by filling it with chicken breasts (bought in bulk or on special offer), fish and a sliced loaf of wholemeal bread (then you'll always be able to make a quick sandwich).
- Steer clear of ready-meals – they're expensive, and many are high in unhealthy ingredients
- Don't buy convenience deli items like pre-packed grated cheese, ready-made fresh sauces and bags of salad leaves. You can prepare them yourself for a fraction of the price
- Keep your store cupboard well stocked so you can always rustle up a quick meal – pasta, tinned tomatoes, brown rice, baked beans, kidney beans, lentils, sardines, tuna and salmon
- Buy spices and herbs in small quantities so you can use them before they go stale

- Cut back on sugary snacks, they won't sustain you
- Keep an eye on your fat intake – that includes butter, cream and cheese
- Don't overdo your intake of nutritional stimulants like coffee, energy drinks, chocolate and cola
- Eat at least five portions of fruit and vegetables each day – and try to eat at least two of them raw

KEEP FOOD FRESH AND SAFE

Most food hygiene is just common sense, but here are a few important reminders:

- Keep your eye on use-by dates on fresh food – throw it away if you don't eat it in time
- If you buy chilled food get it into the fridge as quickly as possible
- Always keep cooked food in the fridge
- Do not leave food in the can once it has been opened – empty it into a small sealable container and keep it in the fridge
- Leftovers should be cooled quickly and put into the fridge – do not put hot food straight into the fridge
- Keep uncooked meat on the lowest shelf and in a deep-sided bowl or dish so it cannot drip onto other food
- Never refreeze food that has been frozen before
- Wash your hands before and after touching food
- Don't try to speed the defrosting process – never defrost chicken or prawns with warm water – you'll risk food poisoning
- When reheating food, make sure it is piping hot – lukewarm food, particularly chicken and pork, could give you food poisoning

The Early 20s

A HOME OF YOUR OWN

Having a home of your own gives you a fantastic opportunity to make a fresh start. Fill the kitchen cupboards, freezer and fridge with all those delicious foods that go towards a healthy diet, and keep temptation at bay by limiting biscuits, cakes and crisps.

If you're moving into a new home, your budget will probably be tight with so much to buy, so start simply and only buy the essentials. Then, if you add a store cupboard item to your shopping trolley each week, you'll soon have everything you need for culinary journeys around the world.

Store-cupboard staples

Packets and pots:
- Wholewheat pasta
- Brown rice
- Wholewheat couscous
- Bulghur wheat
- Red lentils
- 'Small' dried fruit (raisins, etc.)
- Unsalted nuts (of your choice)
- Small packet of flour
- Cornflour
- Salt and pepper
- Small quantity dried parsley
- Small quantity dried chillies
- Curry powder

Tins:
- Chopped plum tomatoes
- Baked beans (reduced-salt, reduced-sugar)
- Sweet corn (in water, no sugar or salt)
- Chickpeas
- Kidney beans

- Cannellini beans
- Tuna in brine
- Sardines or mackerel in brine or tomato sauce
- Salmon
- Fruit in juice

Bottles and jars:
- Olive oil (try to get cold-pressed extra virgin)
- Soy or Tamari sauce
- Mustard
- Vinegar
- Tube tomato puree
- Worcester sauce
- Honey

Freezer
- Peas
- Sweetcorn
- Chicken breasts
- Lean meat
- Loaf of sliced wholemeal bread
- A few wholemeal rolls

FRIDGE STAPLES
There are few fridge essentials apart from a few
items you are likely to use every day, such as:
- Semi-skimmed or skimmed milk
- Low-fat monounsaturated (e.g. olive oil) spread
- Carton of low-fat natural yoghurt or fromage frais
- Salad vegetables
- Eggs

USEFUL EXTRAS
- Fruit spread
- Pesto
- Low-salt vegetable bouillon powder
- Frozen salmon fillets
- Some strong cheese, such as Parmesan
- Dried fruit such as figs or apricots

Make friends with your freezer
As well as helping you to eat healthily, your freezer can save you time
and money. Take advantage of special offers on items such as chicken
breasts, lean meat and salmon fillets, and make double quantities of
dishes and freeze what you don't need immediately.

But remember, some products don't freeze well because of their
composition or texture. Many chilled items cannot be frozen, so
always check the label.

Here are some of the items that don't freeze well:
- Fruit and vegetables: delicate fruit and vegetables and those
  with a high water content – lettuce, celery, cabbage, radishes,
  cucumber and watermelon. Tomatoes, strawberries and
  raspberries do freeze but become soft when they are defrosted
- Cooked egg white: this turns rubbery when frozen, so if you are
  freezing a dish, such as a kedgeree, which contains egg white,
  chop the egg white finely so the rubbery texture is less noticeable
- Thickened sauces and gravies: these may separate as they defrost –
  it's better to freeze the dish with the sauce unthickened, and then
  thicken it after defrosting
- Pasta: slightly undercook your pasta if you plan to freeze a pasta
  dish or the pasta may be too soft after the dish has been reheated
- Potatoes: chunks of potato added to stews and casseroles
  become soft and grainy when frozen – add cooked new potatoes
  to these dishes when you reheat them

Gadgetry and gizmos

Don't go overboard on gadgets. Most of us end up with a motley collection under the stairs or cluttering up the worktops, and seldom, if ever, use them.

Must-have utensils

- Tin opener
- Cheese grater
- Rolling pin
- 2 chopping boards (one reserved for raw meat)
- Garlic press
- Vegetable peeler
- Measuring jug
- Hand whisk
- Potato masher
- Colander
- Metal sieve
- Wooden spoons
- Fish slice
- Kitchen knives
- Set of kitchen scales
- 3 saucepans with lids
- Small and large frying pan
- Roasting tin
- Baking sheet
- Lidded casserole dish
- Kettle
- Toaster

The following items are not essential but very useful to have in the kitchen:

- A microwave – for cooking and quick reheating
- A wok – to knock up healthy stir-fries in minutes
- A blender – for smoothies and milkshakes
- An electric mixer – to knock up healthy cakes and bakes

If you can afford one luxury gadget, or someone would like to buy you a present, go for a 'café' sandwich press. These mini-versions of the machines that turn out those delicious toasted sandwiches and ciabattas at coffee shops allow you to make a great quick meal with a salad.

'If you can afford one luxury gadget, or someone would like to buy you a present, go for a 'café' sandwich press'

Healthy Lunches

Whether you're at work or studying, choosing a healthy lunch will help sustain you through the afternoon without resorting to unhealthy snacks.

Do:

- If you're buying or making a sandwich go for wholemeal or granary bread, or ring the changes with wholemeal pittas, rolls and wraps
- Choose a low-fat protein filling like chicken or turkey topped with a good helping of salad vegetables – steer clear of creamy mayonnaise and dressings
- Go for a protein-rich fish, prawn or chicken salad with a small wholemeal roll – it's a good alternative to a sandwich, but watch the dressings, as bought salads can be high in fat (it's much better to make your own if you can)
- Try a flask of home-made vegetable soup and a wholemeal roll at lunchtime
- Make sure you include at least one piece of fruit or raw vegetables with your lunch – both if possible – it'll help you reach your 5-a-day
- Try to take a break from your desk at lunchtime – if it's a fine day make for the nearest park to get some fresh air

Don't:

- Choose the same lunch every day – variety is the watchword for a balanced healthy diet
- Assume that every 'healthy' or 'skinny' muffin or flapjack is exactly that – check the calorie, sugar and fat content on the label yourself
- Be tempted by lunchtime 'meal deals' if they include unhealthy options like crisps and fizzy drinks

WHEN IT COMES TO A BOUGHT SANDWICH, WRAP OR PITTA, WHAT IS HEALTHY?

Try to choose one containing:

- Less than 5g fat
- Less than 3g saturated fat
- Less than 1.5g salt

A FEW SANDWICH IDEAS

If you really want to be in control, make your own sandwiches. If you use a moist sandwich filling, you won't need any spread.

- Sliced hard-boiled egg seasoned with freshly ground black pepper with lettuce, cucumber and tomato slices
- Cooked sliced chicken with salad vegetables and pickle
- Canned salmon, drained and skin removed, mashed with a splash of vinegar, freshly ground black pepper and a teaspoon of natural fromage frais, with slices of cucumber and shredded lettuce
- Low-fat cream cheese, banana slices and a drizzle of honey
- Cottage cheese and pineapple, drained well, with grated apple and carrot

Alcohol

Alcohol can be both a tonic and a poison. A little can help you to enjoy life and live longer, but too much can kill you. As far as health is concerned, alcohol walks a fine balancing act.

We all know that a glass of wine with a meal, as well as complementing the tastes of the food, can help us to relax and socialise.

But drinking a moderate amount of alcohol can also:
- Reduce your risk of heart disease and stroke by up to 40 per cent
- Increase your level of the 'good' kind of cholesterol, called HDL cholesterol (see page 139)
- Reduce your risk of dangerous thromboses (blood clots)
- Possibly reduce your risk of gallstones

Most of the benefit seems to be due to phytochemicals called phenolics, found especially in red wine, but also in other wines, and even cider.

But there's a tipping point beyond which alcohol causes more harm than good. In the short term, too much booze can:
- Increase your risk of accidents due to impaired judgement
- Cause insomnia and disturbed sleep patterns
- Have dangerous interactions with prescription and other medicines
- Deplete your body of nutrients, especially the B-vitamins, vitamin C and zinc

And that's not even mentioning the horrendous hangover you'll get if you overindulge!

'We all know that a glass of wine with a meal, as well as complementing the tastes of the food, can help us to relax and socialise'

In the long term, the potential for damage is even worse:

- Alcoholism
- Liver damage
- Weight gain and obesity
- Increased risk of heart disease, including heart rhythm disturbances
- Increased risk of oesophagus, mouth and larynx cancer, and possibly liver, bowel and breast cancer
- Increased risk of type-2 diabetes
- Stomach problems
- Depression
- Sexual and fertility problems

The magic level

So, how much alcohol is safe, and how much should you drink for it to actually be good for you?

Moderate drinking is the key:

- Maximum 21 units of alcohol per week for women
- Maximum 28 units of alcohol per week for men
- No more than 2–3 units per day for women, and 3–4 for men
- At least 2 alcohol-free days per week

ARE YOU A BINGE DRINKER?

People often think you have to be 'out of your head' with alcohol to be a binge drinker, but that's not the case. A woman who drinks just over two large glasses of wine in an evening is 'binge' drinking. The official definition is 'more than twice the recommended amount of alcohol at a sitting'.

Problems occur due to confusion over the varying strengths of different kinds of alcoholic drink, and the increasing sizes of pub and restaurant measures served as 'standard'. For example, a unit of alcohol is equivalent to a 125ml glass of wine, but many bars serve 175ml glasses as standard, and large 250ml glasses are increasingly popular. Cans of lager and beer often contain about three-quarters of a pint, rather than half, and so will contain one and a half units, and up to two if it's a high-strength product. Cocktails can be deceptively potent – an innocent-looking glass can easily contain four units. And 'home measures' are notoriously generous!

A recent poll suggested that one in three British men and one in five women binge drink regularly, but almost 70 per cent said they would not classify themselves as binge drinkers.

What's a unit?

- Half a pint of average-strength beer, lager or cider (3–4 per cent alcohol by volume)
- Small (125ml) glass of wine (9 per cent alcohol by volume)
- Standard pub measure (25ml) of spirits (40 per cent alcohol by volume)
- Standard pub measure (50ml) of fortified wine, e.g. sherry, port (20 per cent alcohol by volume)

'A recent poll suggested that one in three British men and one in five women binge drink regularly'

Live well tip

If you don't drink alcohol, there's no need to start – you can still get all the health benefits to your heart and circulatory system from healthy oils, fruit, vegetables and plenty of exercise.

BOOZE AND CALORIES

A few alcoholic drinks in an evening can quickly tot up the calories. Alcohol is packed with calories – only fat has more. And, since alcohol can make you lose your inhibitions and self-restraint, you're more likely to forget about your healthy eating intentions, so a boozy meal out can deal a double-whammy to your waistline!

● A medium glass of wine accounts for 117–165 calories, depending on whether it's dry or sweet (sweet is more calorific)
● A measure of spirits, such as rum, vodka, gin, brandy or whisky, is generally around 52 calories
● A measure of liqueur, such as Tia Maria, Cointreau or Drambuie, accounts for around 66 calories
● Cream liqueurs are slightly higher, at around 81 calories
● A pint of beer ranges from around 142 calories for mild to a hefty 210 for stout
● Cider contains 190–220 calories per pint, depending on whether it's dry or sweet (sweet is more calorific)
● Beware 'premium' and 'extra-strength' beers, ciders and lagers – their calorie count is very variable, and high

BIG ISSUE –
Fatigue And Stress

Have you ever felt that you're a hamster running on a wheel, wearing yourself to exhaustion and never getting anywhere? Most of us would agree that modern life is stressful, but, if we allow the situation to get out of hand, long-term stress doesn't just make us feel rough, it can also raise our blood pressure, increase our risk of heart attacks and stroke, and suppress our immune systems so we're more vulnerable to illness.

We all know we ought to address our stressful lifestyles – learn to relax, take more 'me time'. But did you know that healthy eating is also vital in your anti-stress armoury? If you're stressed, anxious and tired all the time, it might not just be your lifestyle that's at fault – your diet could also be to blame.

When you're feeling tired and stressed, eating healthily is often the last thing on your mind. But this is the time when tasty, nutritious food is just what you need to give you lasting energy and calm your frazzled nerves.

All too often people turn to foody 'crutches' when the going gets tough:

- Sugary snacks
- Stimulants
- Convenience food
- Alcohol
- 'Comfort food'

Sugary snacks

When we're under pressure, we're more likely to skip meals and let our blood-sugar levels drop, until we're absolutely famished. We know that a chocolate muffin or handful of biscuits will give us the energy hit we need, and it's all too easy to ignore the fact that after the initial 'sugar rush' we'll feel low and hungry again. After all, we can always grab another chocolate bar . . .

When you rely on sweet snacks rather than healthy meals for fuel, you're starving your body of nutrients (not to mention playing havoc with your teeth and your waistline!). Your health will suffer.

Don't let yourself get so hungry that only a sugar hit will do. Instead, eat regular meals, based around low-fat protein and wholegrain carbohydrates, with plenty of vegetables to fill you up.

Stimulants

Stimulants, like coffee, tea, cola and energy drinks, can make us feel pleasantly alert. They can also make us feel twitchy, irritable and anxious – just what we least need when under stress. Caffeine also disturbs sleep, so can leave you tired and irritable.

If you think you're using caffeine as a crutch – stop! Step back and realise that it's actually making you feel more stressed, and cut it down, or out. Instead of coffee, try tea (slightly lower in caffeine), rooibos (redbush) tea, herbal tea or 'grain' coffee substitutes.

Convenience foods

When we're feeling hassled, we're more likely to grab convenience foods, and these are generally made from highly processed, refined ingredients. Processing and refining often strips foods of vitamins and minerals, leaving us poorly nourished. At the same time, much of the fibre content is lost, so our meals are less likely to sustain us, leaving us vulnerable to the between-meals munchies.

Comfort foods

Ice cream, pizza, chocolate . . . No one ever says their comfort food is broccoli! Generally, the foods we turn to when we feel the world is against us are dripping with fat, calories and sugar.

This isn't what your poor, stressed body really wants. Try to resist the call of the cookies (it's not easy, but realise that a lot of your craving is down to habit), and comfort yourself with non-food rewards, like cuddling your cat, curling up with a hot drink and a good book, a trip to the cinema, or a country walk with the dog.

STRESS – THE NUTRIENT SAPPER

When you're stressed, you run down your levels of nutrients very rapidly, making it important to keep them topped up.

Some vitamins and minerals are drained particularly rapidly:
- B-vitamins: Your body needs plenty of B-vitamins to cope with stress, but when you're under pressure you use more of these nutrients than ever – make sure you eat plenty of wholegrain foods, lean meat, green leafy vegetables
- Magnesium: Deficiency in magnesium is also associated with low mood, so make sure you're eating enough – good sources include almonds, fish and green leafy vegetables
- Vitamin C: Top up with fresh citrus fruits and juices

BALANCE YOUR ENERGY LEVELS

- Eat little and often – try to have three moderate-sized meals and a couple of healthy snacks, rather than two enormous gorging sessions
- Never skip breakfast, and try always to include some protein and some fruit
- Always have a snack of a piece of fruit and a few nuts to hand for times when you feel your blood sugar dipping – this will gently raise your blood-sugar level, and sustain you until your next meal
- Avoid sugary foods wherever possible
- Eat wholegrain rather than refined (white) carbohydrates
- Cut down your caffeine intake

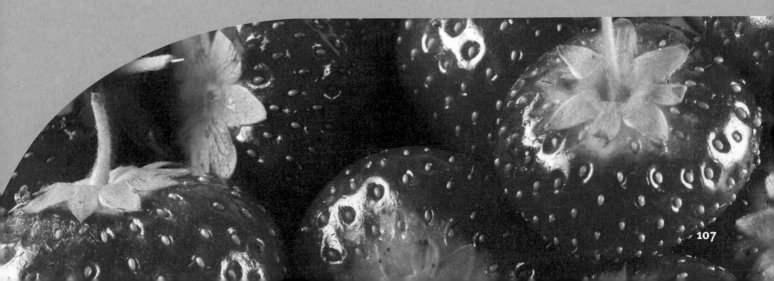

Exercise For Young People

Eating a balanced diet is only one side of the healthy-living equation. Young children and teenagers need at least an hour of physical activity each day.

WHY EXERCISE?

As well as being healthy for children and young people, exercise helps them to:

- Increase their confidence, thanks to learning new skills
- Improve their co-ordination, balance, flexibility and motor skills
- Make new friends
- Learn the benefits of teamwork
- Appreciate that it's participation, not winning, that matters

Most young children enjoy being active – it's often hard to keep them still – but as they get older the lure of computer games and television becomes too much for many of them to resist. So you may need to use a little ingenuity to get them moving. With so many children being driven to school rather than walking or cycling, it's particularly important to build regular exercise into their day.

Don't assume that all the exercise they need is being provided at school. Today less than 50 per cent of children get more than two hours of PE a week – and teenagers often get less. You also have to deduct from that meagre two hours the time that it takes the children to get changed.

Children often say they don't like exercise, perhaps because they believe they're not good at it, or they don't like the competitive side of team games. But they'll be happy to run about in the park for hours on end playing tag or hide and seek, because they consider that 'play' not 'exercise'. So it's all a question of developing an active lifestyle for the whole family and helping children to find physical activities they enjoy. And there are literally scores to choose from.

It's true that participation in some sports activities can be expensive and not everyone has a convenient sports centre or swimming pool, but there are many low-cost or free alternatives. It's always worth checking out your local authority, community centre, after-school or Saturday club facilities. If you're looking for a class in your area, try the local library – they often have extensive lists of what's available for all age groups.

Once you have found out what's on offer and practical for you, involve your child in deciding which sports and activities they'd like to try. They are likely to take part with enthusiasm if they have some input into what they do.

Remember there are many ways to be active, and try to give your children the chance to experience as many as possible. Young children and those who don't like the competitive pressures associated with some sports will be more suited to activities they can do on their own or with like-minded friends.

BUILDING BONES

Weight-bearing exercise is important for building strong bones during childhood and young adulthood, as the best time to build bone density is during years of rapid growth.

Experts recommend that youngsters should get some bone-building exercise at least twice a week. Exercises include:
- Walking
- Running or jogging
- Skipping
- Tennis
- Football
- Netball

Basically, it's any exercise you do standing up and moving about.

GETTING ACTIVE THROUGH THE AGES

The young ones

Under-nines love dashing around, so it's generally not difficult to keep them active – they can get a large proportion of the exercise they need from playing in the garden or in the playground. But if you can walk them to school and home again, or park the car a short distance away and walk the remainder, it will give all of you some extra exercise. Also, if there's a convenient park or playground on the way home, stop off for half an hour so they can let off steam. (Remember to take some water and a healthy snack with you, as they're sure to say they're starving when they come out of school.)

It's still a good idea to look around to see what organised activities are available for their age group, to give them a wider range of activities and opportunities to interact with other children – especially important if they are an only child. But beware of filling their every free moment with organised activities – children need to have time to 'chill out' and perhaps just read a book.

Stealthy exercise

There are plenty of tasks around the house that will help children to get active. Give them one or two to do each week.

Depending on their age and ability why not get them to:
- Help with the vacuuming
- Sweep the patio
- Help clean the windows
- Clean the car
- Mow the lawn
- Water the garden
- Pick up the leaves
- Weed a patch of garden
- Clean their room

Make it easy for little ones to make the most of their 'free' exercise time by having a range of home play equipment to hand, such as skipping ropes, bats and balls, space hoppers, hula hoops, Frisbees, pogo sticks and quoits. And, if you've got a solid flat surface in your garden, why not let them paint or chalk a hopscotch grid?

Pre-teens and early teens

This is often the time when young people lose their way when it comes to keeping active, as exercise will have to compete with the TV, computer games and the Internet. Many children will find a thousand things they need to do, rather than exercise. But, if they've enjoyed physical activity in the past, you should be able to ease them back on track if you can find new and enjoyable sports for them to try.

Think about:
- Archery
- Fencing
- Karate
- Judo
- Horse riding
- Indoor rock climbing
- Dance
- Gymnastics
- Athletics
- Basketball
- Badminton
- Tennis
- Volleyball

Older teens

Older teenagers will tell you it is impossible to fit exercise into their busy schedules – particularly if they spend most of their free time lounging in their room with a computer mouse in one hand and a mobile phone in the other.

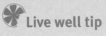 **Live well tip**

Get in the swim – this is one important (and potentially life-saving) activity you should consider. If you don't feel confident to teach your child to swim yourself, most local swimming pools have classes for children. If you can't swim yourself, why not sign up for a class too – it will soon be another activity you can enjoy together.

Joking aside, it can often be difficult for them to juggle the demands of lectures, essays, visits to the college library and, if they're living away from home, their shopping, cooking and washing. But it is still important that they keep physically active – experts believe that older teenagers should aim for some physical activity every day and at least three twenty-minute, and two thirty-minute, sessions of more vigorous exercise each week.

Teenagers who have enjoyed team sports and physical activity throughout their lives will have no difficulty finding teams to join, and even new sports to try, at school and college. It is the more reluctant exercisers, who might think that at last they have a legitimate reason to ease off, who need all the encouragement they can get. This is the age when many teenagers drop out of organised sport, so it is important that parents try to suggest other activities to take their place.

They might like to try something a bit different, so how about:
- Yoga or Pilates
- Paintball
- Dry-slope skiing
- Ice skating
- Mountain biking
- Windsurfing
- Rollerblading
- Kick boxing
- Jogging
- Water polo
- Ice hockey

. . . or any from the list for younger teenagers that they haven't tried.

Teenage girls may enjoy an exercise or dance class (the variety is endless, from jive to modern, and salsa to belly dancing), and teenage boys might like a chance to use equipment at a gym – many local authorities and schools have gyms, so they don't need to join an expensive private club.

Think about . . .

We've been talking about how you can eat healthily when you're at your youngest. But even if you're still in the first Lifestage, you should nevertheless be thinking ahead, and considering how the food you eat affects:

- Blood pressure and cholesterol levels (see page 138) – are you eating too much salt or saturated fat?
- Cancer prevention (see page 151) – are you getting enough fruit and vegetables?
- Body weight (see page 130) – are you eating more calories than you use?
- Digestion (see page 212) – do you eat enough fibre?
- Osteoporosis (see page 191) – is your diet high enough in calcium?
- Mental decline (see page 198) – have you tried green tea?
- Your joints (see page 188) – do you get enough 'good fats' in your diet?

Life Stage 2

you are™
what
you eat™

Healthy Eating Through Your 20s, 30s And 40s

At this stage of our life we may encounter undreamed-of independence and new opportunities – the world's our oyster! But it can also herald the start of the busiest time of our lives as we struggle to juggle a career, a hectic social life, family and new responsibilities. So it's easy to see why it's important to find the time to make the right decisions about our diet and lifestyle now. If we avoid the pitfalls of a poor diet, meals on the run, snatched sleep and lack of exercise, we'll reap the rewards for the rest of our lives.

HEALTHY EATING FOR PLANNING A BABY

Healthy nutrition is vital when you're planning a baby.

At least three months (and preferably six months) before you intend to conceive, you should:

- Be eating a good, wholefood diet – low-fat protein, energy from starchy carbohydrates (preferably wholegrains), a moderate amount of 'healthy' fats, and plenty of fruit and vegetables
- Be at your optimum weight – mothers who are under- or overweight are less likely to conceive, more likely to suffer difficulties in pregnancy such as high blood pressure and gestational diabetes, and more at risk from birth complications
- Ensure you're fit and healthy to start with – the nine months of pregnancy puts a considerable strain on your body
- Make sure your diet contains the full range of vitamins and minerals, for trouble-free ovulation and conception

- Ensure you're eating enough of the nutrients needed for the earliest stages of your baby's development
- Be careful not to eat or drink anything that could harm your baby

Because the crucial first stages of your baby's development take place before you even know you're pregnant, you need to have sufficient supplies of certain vitamins and minerals in place to supply the embryo's requirements.

TOP NUTRIENTS FOR PLANNING A BABY

Folic acid

Folic acid is so important in the early stages of pregnancy, all women are advised to take a supplement of 400mcg (micrograms) from the time they start trying to conceive and for the first twelve weeks of pregnancy.

This is because folic acid is needed for the formation of the baby's nervous system, and a deficiency of this B-vitamin can increase your baby's risk of suffering a neural tube defect such as spina bifida. You should also eat plenty of foods rich in folic acid, such as brown rice and green leafy vegetables.

Omega-3 and omega-6 essential fatty acids

Omega essential fatty acids are vital for the formation of the brain and nervous system, which begins between two and three weeks after conception. Both omega-3 and omega-6 EFAs are important but, since omega-6s are much more common in the diet, women planning a baby should concentrate on increasing their intake of omega-3s, from oily fish (up to two portions per week), and flaxseeds and their oil.

Zinc

This mineral is needed for the production of sex hormones, and for ovulation and fertility in women. Oysters are the best source (hence their 'sexy' reputation as an aphrodisiac), but you can also get zinc from other shellfish, meat, fish, eggs, or nuts and seeds (especially pumpkin seeds).

A HEALTHY DIET FOR DAD

The future father's diet is important too, in order to produce top-quality sperm.

Sperm cells take about three months to mature, so it's important for men to take a good look at their diets well in advance.

- Eat a nutritious diet based around wholefoods – to provide all the building blocks for healthy sperm
- Maintain a healthy weight – being overweight or underweight hampers your fertility
- Get plenty of zinc, from seafood, lean meat and seeds – deficiency leads to reduced fertility and low sperm counts
- Cut down on alcohol – it saps your zinc levels
- Watch your selenium intake – deficiency can reduce your sperm count (the best selenium source is Brazil nuts)

'Oysters are the best source of zinc but you can also get it from other shellfish, meat, fish, eggs, or nuts and seeds'

Healthy Eating For Pregnancy

The nine months you spend in the womb have arguably the biggest impact on your health for the rest of your life. This is when the first seeds of good health – or not – are sown.

The food a pregnant woman eats has an immense effect on her baby's development. An expectant mum's diet even affects her baby's chance of developing high blood pressure, heart disease, stroke and type-2 diabetes when he or she grows up.

A developing baby has unique nutritional needs, and has to obtain all of them from its mother, so the expectant mum has increased requirements for many nutrients.

If you're undernourished, your chances of conceiving fall dramatically. If you are severely underweight, you may not be ovulating, in which case you certainly won't be able to become pregnant.

You don't have to 'eat for two' in terms of quantity – too many calories can lead to putting on an unhealthy amount of weight. For the first six months, you don't need to eat any extra, and only an additional 200 calories a day for the third trimester of pregnancy.

But a woman's vitamin and mineral needs double when she is pregnant – after all, she has to supply all the growing baby's requirements too – so it's a good idea to think that you're eating for two in terms of quality.

So, even when you do need to eat more towards the end of your pregnancy, make those extra calories really count in terms of nutrients. Don't squander them on a sticky cake or Danish pastry – far better to have an open sandwich made with a slice of wholemeal bread and some turkey and salad – full of low-fat protein, slow-release carbohydrates and vitamins, especially the B-vitamins.

Because of the extra needs of the unborn baby, a pregnant woman's body becomes super-efficient at absorbing nutrients from her food. This is fortunate, because the baby is very 'selfish' as far as its nutrition is concerned, and will 'steal' vitamins and minerals from its mother's body in order to supply its own developmental requirements.

So you can see how important it is to get the very best diet you can while you're expecting, to keep you strong and healthy during your pregnancy, and to provide your growing baby with all the nutrients it needs.

TOP NUTRIENTS FOR PREGNANT MUMS

Protein

Pregnant women need a little extra protein – protein is required to build new body cells. But the extra needed is small, only a few grams per day. Concentrate on making sure the protein you eat is high quality – sources such as beans and lentils, fish, lean meat and poultry are ideal.

Folic acid

Pregnant women need extra folic acid, for the formation of the baby's nervous system during the early stages of pregnancy. Pregnant women should continue to take a 400mcg folic acid supplement for the first twelve weeks of pregnancy, to reduce the risk of their baby having a spinal cord defect such as spina bifida. If you are at higher risk of giving birth to a baby with a neural tube defect (for example, you already have a child with spina bifida), your doctor will probably prescribe a higher-dose supplement for you.

Even after the first trimester, expectant mums should eat a diet rich in folic acid, with plenty of green vegetables, pulses, brown rice, nuts and fortified breakfast cereals.

Iron

You need iron to make red blood cells, to carry oxygen around your body. You need *more* red blood cells too – your body makes as much as 50 per cent more blood during pregnancy. The baby also needs iron to build its own red blood cells. If you don't get enough iron in your diet (and particularly if your iron stores were low before you became pregnant), you could become anaemic, with symptoms of tiredness, weakness and poor concentration.

The best, most useable, sources of iron are animal products such as lean red meat and eggs, but iron is also found in non-animal foods such as beans and lentils, nuts, dried fruits, green vegetables and fortified breakfast cereals. Drink some vitamin-C-rich orange juice with your meals to ensure you absorb the maximum iron.

Don't overdo the red meat during pregnancy, despite its iron-rich qualities, as it is high in saturated fat. And, although liver is a fantastic source of iron, you should avoid it during pregnancy.

Calcium

All the calcium needed to build a baby's bones must come from its mother's diet, so it's important for her to eat enough calcium-rich foods to supply both their needs. Although your body's ability to absorb calcium from your diet becomes super-efficient, if you don't get enough, your baby will take calcium from your calcium stores in order to supply its own requirements.

Unless dairy gives you problems, eating or drinking three portions of low-fat dairy products a day is an excellent way for pregnant mums to get their calcium. Other good sources of calcium are canned fish where the bones are eaten, such as salmon and sardines (also great for omega-3s), green vegetables and sesame seeds.

As well as calcium, you'll also need sufficient vitamin D in order to absorb it from your diet. Fifteen minutes of sunlight on your skin every day during the sunny months enables your body to make and store its own vitamin D, but if this isn't possible for you, or you have dark skin (which is less efficient at making the vitamin) or cover your skin when you go out, you can also get vitamin D from oily fish, eggs, dairy products, and low-fat spreads that are fortified with the vitamin.

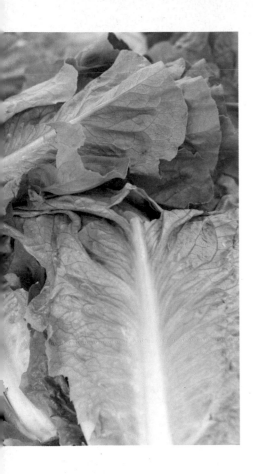

Nutrient focus – Calcium

Calcium is the 'bones and teeth' mineral.

Your calcium needs are highest during periods of rapid bone building – during childhood and adolescence, and also during pregnancy, when the baby's bones are being formed. Breast-feeding mothers also have very high calcium requirements.

We only gain bone mass up until the age of around thirty. Beyond that, bone is constantly being remodelled and replaced, and soon you're breaking down bone faster than you can rebuild it. Calcium is gradually lost, increasing our risk of the bone-thinning disease osteoporosis. This makes it particularly important to build up strong bones in the first three decades of life, to build up a good 'bone bank' to offset the later effect of ageing.

About 1.5kg of your body weight is calcium, and all but 15g of this is in your bones and teeth. The small remainder, which circulates in your blood, is nonetheless vital, as it is involved in a variety of body processes, including making your muscles contract, helping to regulate your blood pressure, allowing your blood to clot when you're injured and enabling your nervous system to function properly.

In order for your body to absorb and use calcium, you need sufficient vitamin D (which you can get from the action of sunlight on the skin, or by eating fish or dairy products).

The best food sources of calcium are milk and other dairy products and, handily enough, they also provide vitamin D to help the absorption of this bone-friendly mineral, and phosphorus, which is also needed to build healthy bones. The lactose (milk sugar) in milk is also thought to enhance calcium absorption. If you're a vegan, or can't drink milk, then tofu, sesame seeds, dried fruits, nuts and green leafy vegetables also provide a supply of the mineral.

As well as vitamin D, it's thought that magnesium, phosphorus and vitamin K are also needed to get the most from your calcium and build healthy bones. Good sources include lean meat, low-fat dairy products and green vegetables (for magnesium), and eggs and fish oils (for vitamin K).

CALCIUM ENEMIES

Some foods can block your absorption of calcium, or leach it from your bones.

- Fibre: hinders the absorption of calcium from food
- Tea: tannins in tea bind with calcium in the gut, so that it can't be absorbed
- Caffeine: there's some evidence that the caffeine in drinks such as coffee, tea and cola can increase excretion of calcium from the body
- Fizzy drinks: the phosphoric acid in carbonated drinks can decrease the uptake of calcium from food

Vitamin A

You need enough vitamin A for your baby's healthy development, but too much can be harmful. For this reason pregnant women are advised not to eat liver (the richest source of vitamin A) or to take vitamin A supplements or cod-liver oil supplements (as these are also very high in the vitamin). If you are struggling with your vitamin and mineral intake while you're pregnant, your doctor may advise you to take a supplement specifically designed for pregnancy, which won't contain an overly high level of vitamin A.

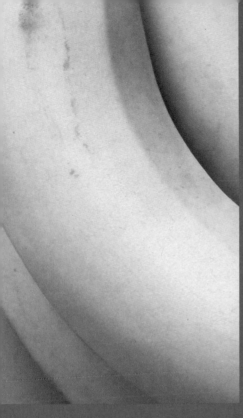

Fibre

Constipation can be a problem during pregnancy, and eating fibre-rich foods can help to prevent and relieve it, along with drinking plenty of water. Go for fruit and vegetables, beans and lentils, and plenty of wholegrains like brown rice, wholemeal pasta and wholemeal bread.

ESSENTIAL FATTY ACIDS

The brain is over two-thirds fat, and an important proportion of this is the omega-3 and omega-6 essential fatty acids, especially the omega-3s called DHA and EPA (up to 40 per cent of each brain cell's fat content is DHA). When the baby's brain is developing, if the mother's diet isn't supplying it with enough omega-3, it will use omega-6 instead, which is less suitable for brain building. This makes it particularly important for pregnant women to get enough omega-3, especially in the third trimester of pregnancy, when the baby's brain is growing and forming new connections at its fastest rate.

Pregnant women should try to eat two portions of oily fish (the best source of omega-3s) a week, but not more, because these fish can contain heavy-metal toxins, which could harm the baby in high concentrations.

DON'T TRY TO 'SLIM'

Although you should be careful not to put on too much extra weight during your pregnancy, never be tempted to go on a 'slimming' diet while you're pregnant, for example if you're worried about getting your figure back after the birth. Cutting back on food is likely to compromise your intake of the nutrients both you and your baby desperately need during this crucial time.

The average weight gain during pregnancy is 10–12kg (22–28lb), but expectant mums gain weight at different rates. Just because you're gaining faster or slower than someone else, it doesn't mean anything is amiss. Ask your doctor or midwife for advice about the weight you should be gaining.

WHAT *NOT* TO EAT
You also need to steer clear of foods that could harm your baby.

Alcohol
It's incredibly easy for alcohol to cross over from your bloodstream to your baby's, putting the baby at risk from delayed development, birth defects and premature birth. Heavy drinking during pregnancy can cause Foetal Alcohol Syndrome – a collection of potentially fatal birth defects that include low birth weight, retardation and heart defects. The official guidelines say pregnant women shouldn't drink more than one or two units of alcohol, once or twice a week. But recent research suggests that, even at lower alcohol intakes, drinking alcohol during pregnancy can be riskier to the unborn baby than previously thought.

If at all possible, you should give up alcohol completely before you plan to conceive, because the foetus is at its most vulnerable during the first few weeks of pregnancy, before you know you're pregnant.

Caffeine
You don't have to cut out caffeine completely while you're pregnant, but it's a good idea to cut down. At any rate, you shouldn't drink more than 300mg per day, as higher levels can lead to low birth weight and even miscarriage. Caffeine can also disrupt your sleep, leaving you tired and adding to the fatigue experienced by many women during pregnancy.

There is a table of the amount of caffeine in different foods and drinks on page 51, but, to give you a rough idea, 300mg is the amount found in three mugs of instant coffee or six cups of tea.

FOOD POISONING RISKS
Some foods should be avoided because they could give you food poisoning or harm your baby:
- Raw and lightly cooked eggs
- Undercooked meat or poultry
- Unpasteurised milk
- Paté
- Mould-ripened soft cheeses such as Brie and Camembert
- Blue-veined cheeses such as Stilton and Danish Blue (cottage cheese, cream cheese and hard cheese such as Cheddar are fine)

Certain fish

Pregnant women should avoid eating shark, swordfish and marlin. This is because potentially harmful levels of heavy-metal toxins can build up in their flesh. Although they probably wouldn't harm the mother, they could damage the developing baby.

FOOD CRAVINGS

If you have a food craving while you're pregnant, should you give in? A craving could possibly be due to your body 'knowing' that it needs a particular nutrient, but certainly not all cravings are for foods your body needs.

You need to use your common sense. If your craving is for a banana or some pickled onions (or even both together!), it won't do you any harm to succumb. But if you're desperate for a bag of doughnuts, be firm with yourself and have something that provides the taste satisfaction you want (a currant bun, for example), but with less of the unhealthy side effects.

PEANUT PRECAUTION

If the baby's mother, father, brothers or sisters suffer from allergies (such as food allergies, hay fever, asthma or eczema), the baby is more likely to develop a peanut allergy if they're exposed to peanut allergens in the womb or through their mother's milk.

Because of this, it's best to avoid eating peanuts when you're pregnant or breast-feeding, if you or a close relative have an allergy of any kind.

Healthy Eating For Breast-feeding

When you're producing milk for your baby, you'll need extra nutrients, notably:

- Protein
- Calcium
- Iron
- Magnesium
- Zinc
- Vitamin A
- Vitamin C
- Omega-3 essential fatty acids

You'll also need more calories – around 2,500 a day in total. Make every calorie count in nutritional terms (no junk food!) to help you reach your nutrient targets.

It's also easy to become dehydrated when you're breast-feeding – you'll need to drink more water than your usual 1.5–2-litre requirement. If you notice your urine is dark in colour, you're not drinking enough.

KEY NUTRIENTS FOR BREAST-FEEDING

Protein

You'll require extra protein, because you'll be using up a lot in order to produce milk. You don't need a huge amount – you can make up your extra requirement with 150ml of semi-skimmed milk, 100ml of low-fat yoghurt or 20g of chicken breast.

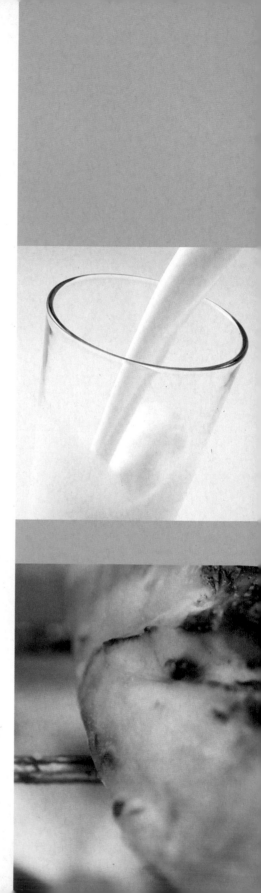

FOODS TO AVOID

Many things in a mother's diet can be passed on to her baby through her milk, so you should follow these rules:

- Avoid shark, swordfish and marlin (see pages 18-19)
- Don't eat more than two portions of oily fish a week
- Cut down on caffeine
- Avoid alcohol
- Avoid peanuts if there is a family history of allergy
- Ask your doctor or pharmacist before taking any medicines, even over-the-counter medicines

Calcium

Breast-feeding requires a lot of calcium – almost double the amount needed during your pregnancy. You'll be passing about 250mg a day on to your baby through your milk, which is almost a third of an adult's usual daily requirement! If you don't get enough in your diet, the shortfall will be drawn from your bones, so breast-feeding women are advised to include five servings of dairy products in their diet each day, to ensure they reach their calcium target.

Iron

After your pregnancy, your iron stores may be depleted, so it's important to top up this important mineral. A deficiency can leave you feeling weak and tired, just when you need all your energy to care for your new baby.

Omega-3 essential fatty acids

These brain-healthy fats are passed on to your baby during pregnancy and through your milk when you're breast-feeding. It's important to keep up your intake, to provide a good supply for your baby, and top up your own stores (which the baby may have depleted during your pregnancy). Studies suggest that babies whose mothers didn't eat enough omega-3s lagged behind better-nourished children in terms of brain development, and were more likely to show behavioural disorders such as ADHD. The differences became particularly obvious when the children started school.

To get plenty of omega-3s, you should try to eat two portions of oily fish a week – but not more, since they can contain low levels of toxins, which nonetheless could be harmful to your baby. Another omega-3 source is flaxseeds (and their oil), though this form of the healthy fat is harder for the body to use.

BIG ISSUE –
Overweight And Obesity

Are you worried about your weight? If so, you're not alone – at any one time an estimated 40 per cent of women and 24 per cent of men are trying to lose weight.

The UK (and much of the developed world) is in the grip of an obesity epidemic and, if you're a healthy weight, you're in the fortunate minority:

- 62 per cent of men and 53 per cent of women are overweight
- 17 per cent of men and 20 per cent of women are obese (seriously overweight)

And the situation looks set to get worse – the latest government predictions expect that about a third of adults (and a fifth of all children) will be obese by 2010.

WHY IS IT A PROBLEM?

Being overweight, particularly if you're unfit as well, is no laughing matter, as it seriously increases your risk of several serious diseases:

- High blood pressure
- Increased blood cholesterol
- Heart disease
- Stroke
- Type-2 diabetes
- Certain cancers, such as uterus, breast, bowel and kidney cancer
- Degenerative brain diseases such as Alzheimer's

Being overweight also increases the strain on your joints, so you're more susceptible to aches and pains, and osteoarthritis. Obesity even hampers sperm production in men, and makes it harder for women to conceive.

WHY DO PEOPLE PUT ON WEIGHT?

It's a straightforward formula:
- If you regularly eat more calories than you use up, your body stores them, and you put on weight
- If you regularly burn more calories (through physical activity) than you take in, you lose weight
- If the calories you take in equal the calories you burn up, you maintain your weight

HOW HAVE THINGS GOT SO BAD?

We haven't suddenly become overweight and obese simply through eating too much – it's actually down to what the scientists call the 'obesogenic environment':
- Fast food makes calories cheap and quick to eat
- We eat out more, and eat more fattening food when we do
- 'Convenience food' is often high in fat and sugar
- Less of us do manual work, so we burn fewer calories
- We drive more, and walk and cycle less
- Our hobbies involve less exercise

But there's another complication. Muscle burns more energy than fat, so muscular people use up more calories than flabby people. And some people naturally burn up more calories – it's genetic. Also, your health, lifestyle and even your environment affect the amount of calories you burn.

Losing weight is simply a matter of eating fewer calories than you expend. And that doesn't mean starving yourself – if you feel hungry and deprived your willpower is much more likely to crumble.

The way to lose weight – and keep it off – isn't a fad diet. They don't work. You need to change your whole way of eating, for good. But it's not complicated – a weight-loss diet isn't much different to a healthy balanced diet for anyone. In other words, what we've been describing throughout this book.

When you need to lose weight you just need to:
- Try to avoid the 'calorie-dense' foods
- Make friends with the 'nutrient-dense' foods
- Keep your portion sizes under control

Calorie-dense foods tend to be those that are high in fat and sugar – think of:
- Fast food
- Sausages and other processed-meat products
- Chips and crisps
- Cakes and biscuits
- Ice cream and chocolate

They may taste good, but they don't really fill you up for long, do they?

But (fortunately for you) the nutrient-dense foods tend to be low in calories, and filling too.

Fruit and vegetables are the slimmer's friend – they fill you up, and (so long as you don't bump up the calorie count with sugar, creamy sauces or butter) they're really low in calories, not to mention packed full of vitamins, minerals and phytochemicals.

But that doesn't mean that eating to lose weight means living on rabbit food! You can also have:
- Lean meat, poultry, fish and low-fat dairy products – just hold off the fat and sugary sauces and additions, and use low-fat cooking methods, like grilling, poaching, steaming and baking
- Beans and pulses – the ultimate sustainers, thanks to protein and fibre

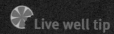 **Live well tip**
Reduce the amount of calories contained in your food – by cutting back on sugar and fat, and keeping your portion sizes under control – while still eating a nutritious, exciting and balanced diet.

- Wholegrain carbohydrates – these provide long-lasting energy
- Moderate amounts of 'good' fats – the healthy mono- and polyunsaturated types – can help your weight loss progress, as they help keep your blood-sugar levels stable

YOU STILL NEED TREATS

No food should be completely off limits, because forbidden foods become irresistible. If chocolate, for example, is banned, you're more likely to succumb to gorging a whole family-sized bar than if you allowed yourself, say, one square of good-quality dark chocolate every couple of days.

That's not to say you shouldn't be aware of which foods are packed with calories. You should try to steer clear of them – just allow yourself to relax, every once in a while, and make up for your indulgence with ultra-healthy eating afterwards. You'll be far more likely to stick to a healthy weight-loss diet if you're not feeling miserable and deprived.

And don't beat yourself up if you lapse, and succumb to an ice cream or some other indulgence you said you'd do without. Just start again – tomorrow is a new day.

DO YOU NEED TO LOSE WEIGHT?

For decades, the usual method for determining whether someone is overweight has been the body mass index, or BMI. This basically compares your weight with your height.

BMI = your weight (in kg) divided by your height (in metres) squared:
- Below 18.5 = underweight
- 18.5 to 25 = healthy weight
- 25 to 29 = overweight
- Over 30 = obese

But for many people, BMI doesn't provide an accurate indication of whether they weigh more than is healthy. BMI isn't accurate if you're pregnant, or a child. And the proportion of your body that's made up of muscle also skews your BMI. Muscle weighs much more than fat, so very fit, healthy muscular types end up in the overweight or obese category. They're heavy because of all that muscle, but they're certainly not flabby. It's not unusual for a sportsman such as a professional rugby player to have a BMI of 32, and you wouldn't want to call him obese, would you?

A better way of determining whether your weight is a risk to your health is to measure your waist and your hips. This is because the *amount* of fat you carry is actually less important than *where* you store it.

Pear-shaped people:
● Store fat around their hips, bottom and thighs
● Are more likely to be women

Apple shaped people:
● Store fat around their waist
● Are more likely to be men

So, how do you know if you're an apple shape, with too much fat around your belly? Take your waist measurement, and divide it by your hip measurement. This is the danger level:
● Ratio over 0.9 for men
● Ratio over 0.85 for women

Fat stored around your middle is more likely to 'escape' into the bloodstream and contribute to high cholesterol levels, heart disease, stroke and diabetes. Unfortunately, there's not a lot a lot you can do about whether you've got a natural tendency to be an apple or a pear – it's mainly down to your genes. But, because of the greater health risks, it's all the more important for 'apples' to shift any extra pounds and inches.

'A good way of determining whether your weight is a risk to your health is to measure your waist and your hips'

For an even quicker way of determining whether you've got a 'killer belly', simply measure your waist. If it's larger than 120cm (40 inches) for a man, or 88cm (35 inches) for a woman, your fat is a hazard to your health.

TIPS TO GET YOU STARTED

If you need to lose weight, here are some tips to help you lose weight slowly and consistently while still eating a healthy diet:

- Keep a food diary to become more aware of your habits and problem areas
- Watch your portion sizes and review them regularly – it's easy to increase them without noticing
- Reduce your intake of fat, especially harmful saturated and trans fats
- Reduce your intake of sugar
- Eat regular meals
- Always eat a good breakfast, including some protein
- Increase your intake of fruit and vegetables
- Use vegetables and fruits as snacks and desserts
- Take at least thirty minutes, moderate exercise each day and aim to build up to sixty minutes on most days
- Be realistic: aim to lose no more than 0.5–1kg (1–2lb) a week – crash diets can be dangerous and aren't sustainable in the long term

THE DIET TRAP

It's easy to be tempted by quick-fix diets promising that the pounds will melt away and stay away. But don't be fooled – faddy diets don't work and they could result in nutrient deficiencies leading to possible anaemia, damage to your bones and harm to your immune system.

Study after study has found that permanent weight loss is only possible through a sensible long-term eating plan. Maintaining a balanced diet while you're losing weight helps you to keep positive (it's no fun existing on cabbage and grapefruit) and ensures that your body gets all the nutrients it requires to stay healthy and active.

WEIGHT LOSS MATHS

The energy content of 0.5kg (1lb) of body fat is 3,500 calories. So to lose 0.5kg in a week you need a calorie deficit of 3,500 calories, or 500 calories each day.

The simplest way to achieve this is to make small changes to the amount of calories you eat and to take more exercise – which will also burn up the calories.

Try these swaps to cut the calories:
- A banana instead of a chocolate bar (150 calorie saving)
- A currant bun instead of a Danish pastry (233 calories saving)
- A virtually fat-free yoghurt instead of a full-fat fruit yoghurt (130 calories saving)

Then add two 15-minute brisk walks (150 calories burned)

Total saving = 663 calories

Carry on like this every day, and you should soon be well on your way to your target weight.

Take a look at your diet and, wherever you can, swap a high-sugar item for a low-sugar item, and a high-fat food for a low-fat one. Also look out for where you can make savings in fat and sugar by choosing reduced-sugar and reduced-fat versions of products such as beans, breakfast cereals, dairy products and preserves when you do your shopping.

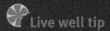
TIPS TO STOP YOU OVEREATING

- Keep your meals and snacks regular. Never go more than five hours without a meal or a snack (except overnight)
- Allow for healthy snacks to keep your blood sugar stable and minimise cravings. Eat a carbohydrate and protein snack one or two hours before your meal, for example an oatcake spread with low-fat cream cheese
- Drink a glass of ice-cold water before you start your meal
- Start your meal with a small salad with no dressing or a reduced-fat dressing, an apple or a bowl of vegetable soup. It will curb your appetite and you will be able to eat less of the main course
- When you're eating out, choose a clear (not creamy) soup for your starter. Then order a starter-sized portion for your main course with extra vegetables. Skip the calorific dessert and have a slice of melon or other fruit instead
- Keep moving. Exercise will take your mind off food and reduce stress

'Start your meal with a small salad with no dressing or a reduced-fat dressing, an apple or a bowl of vegetable soup'

Eat To Beat – Cardiovascular Disease

Cardiovascular disease is heart disease (including heart attacks) and stroke. A stroke is basically a 'brain attack' where a blood clot lodges in the brain, cutting off the blood vessel, or a blood vessel in the brain bursts (a brain or cerebral haemorrhage).

Cardiovascular disease is the main cause of death in the UK, accounting for a massive 40 per cent of all deaths. But there's a lot you can do to reduce your risk by improving your diet and lifestyle.

Heart disease is the most common cause of premature death in the UK, and most of these deaths are due to heart attacks.

THE HEART-HEALTHY DIET

Because heart disease and stroke have the same root causes, what we call a 'heart-healthy diet' reduces your risk of both.

A heart-healthy diet will:

- Help you to maintain your target weight
- Lower your levels of the 'bad' LDL cholesterol that leads to clogged arteries
- Raise your levels of the 'good' HDL cholesterol that removes harmful fats from your bloodstream
- Lower your blood pressure
- Reduce inflammation, which, along with the 'wrong' balance of the two kinds of cholesterol, contributes to clogging of the arteries

Live well tip

To cut your risk of cardiovascular disease:
- Give up smoking
- Maintain a healthy weight
- Eat a heart-healthy diet
- Get a healthy amount of exercise

CHOLESTEROL

People used to get very concerned about the amount of cholesterol they ate, but we now know that dietary cholesterol isn't that critical in determining your overall cholesterol number. Much more important is the cholesterol that your body manufactures itself, in your liver. And the amount your liver churns out is determined by the amount and kind of fat you eat. (Your genes can also play a part – people suffering from a condition called familial hypercholesterolaemia have an inherited tendency to make more cholesterol than is healthy.)

Our bodies need cholesterol to make cell membranes, bile and hormones. It's so important that our livers produce their own supply. It's only too much cholesterol in the wrong place (i.e. our bloodstream and arteries) that's bad news.

There are actually two kinds of cholesterol complexes, which determine how much cholesterol circulates in your bloodstream, and where it ends up. One kind, LDL cholesterol, is dangerous, dumping cholesterol in fatty deposits on our artery walls. The other kind, HDL cholesterol, is good for us, helping to remove harmful fats from the bloodstream.

When the doctor says you need to reduce your cholesterol number, they're talking about your overall level and your LDL level – not your 'good' HDL cholesterol. Having a healthy level of HDL can help to offset the effects of the 'bad' LDL cholesterol.

So, while your LDL cholesterol is furring up your arteries, your HDL is doing its best to keep them clean and clear. And the ratio of LDL to HDL in your blood depends a lot upon what you eat.
- Saturated and trans fats are bad for your cholesterol balance
- Monounsaturated and polyunsaturated fats are good for your cholesterol balance
- Other foods, such as fibre-rich foods, fruit and vegetables, are also good for your cholesterol levels

Watch that weight

Being overweight is a definite heart risk. It places strain on your heart muscle, and increases your levels of artery-clogging harmful cholesterol. Having too much fat increases LDL and decreases HDL, just the reverse of what you want, and this effect seems to be worse in 'apple-shaped' people who store fat around their waist than in 'pear-shapes' who store it on their hips and thighs.

Fruit and vegetables

Fruit and vegetables are rich in antioxidants, which help prevent the oxidation process that leads to damage and 'furring up' of the artery walls. They're also high in potassium, which helps to control blood pressure by counterbalancing the sodium in your blood. Blueberries and prunes are brilliant for antioxidants, and bananas are great for potassium.

Pulses – beans and lentils

Pulses are a good source of protein, they're filling, and extremely low in saturated fat – something you need to minimise in a heart-healthy diet. They're also high in soluble fibre, which 'mops up' harmful cholesterol in the body.

Oily fish

Oily fish, such as salmon, trout, mackerel, sardines, pilchards and fresh tuna, can reduce your risk of cardiovascular disease – most people should aim to eat it two or three times a week. The secret is in the omega-3 essential fatty acids, which improve your cholesterol balance and reduce the risk of dangerous blood clots.

Healthy oils

Replace the saturated and trans fats in your diet with healthier unsaturated fats (polyunsaturates and monounsaturates) to reduce your risk of clogged arteries. Monounsaturated fats, such as olive oil, are great at lowering your levels of the 'bad' LDL cholesterol.

But you still need to watch your total fat intake. If it causes you to put on weight, that will increase your heart risk.

Live well tip
Get moving – exercise boosts your level of healthy HDL cholesterol.

Heart fact
Cultures where a lot of oily fish is eaten, such as the Japanese and Inuit, have lower levels of cardiovascular disease.

Nuts

Studies suggest that eating nuts is good for your cholesterol levels, probably due to their high monounsaturated fat content, along with antioxidant vitamin E, fibre and B-vitamins. Foods rich in vitamin E appear to be particularly effective against heart disease.

High-fibre carbohydrates

'Brown' starchy carbohydrates, like wholemeal bread, wholemeal pasta, brown rice and other wholegrains, are rich in fibre. They also help weight control by filling you up and balancing your blood-sugar levels.

Oats are especially good for your heart – their high soluble fibre content works like a sponge, soaking up excess cholesterol.

Polyphenols

Plant chemicals called polyphenols, found in wine and tea, mount a three-pronged attack on your heart disease risk. They:

- Lower your levels of 'bad' LDL cholesterol, reducing your risk of clogged arteries
- Slightly thin your blood, reducing your risk of dangerous blood clots
- Act as antioxidants, which help to prevent the damage to artery walls that makes 'furring' and blockages more likely

It could be a good idea to replace your usual spread with one high in monounsaturated fats (such as olive oil) and enriched with plant sterols or plant stanols – they've been proven to help lower cholesterol levels.

Red wine and green tea seem to work best, but all wines and teas seem to have some beneficial effect. Just don't overdo the wine, as too much alcohol can have the opposite effect (see below).

Soya protein

Research suggests that replacing animal protein with 50g of soya protein a day can reduce total cholesterol levels by 12 per cent. What's even better is that it reduces your 'bad' LDL cholesterol and increases your 'good' HDL levels. And the oil from soya is the healthy unsaturated kind.

SOYA SENSE

Here are some easy ways to get soya into your diet. You'll find a wide range of products in the supermarket, at Asian grocers and health food shops.

- Use soya milk or soya yoghurt on your breakfast cereal
- Used tinned soya beans in stews and casseroles
- Serve soya ice cream or yoghurt with fresh fruit for dessert
- Look out for bread containing soya flour
- Use soya mince to make Bolognese sauces and savoury mince for cottage pie
- Marinate tofu and use in stir-fries
- Whiz up a banana with soya milk to make a creamy-tasting smoothie
- Ask for your latte or cappuccino to be made with soya milk

 **Live well tip**
Eat garlic – it can help lower your levels of 'bad' LDL cholesterol.

GOJI BERRIES

Could these tiny Himalayan fruits be the next superfood? Goji berries (also called gogi berries) are sold dried and slightly chewy, and are about the size of a raisin. Their taste is said to be sweet, with a hint of saltiness.

Goji berries are very high in antioxidants, especially betacarotene and vitamin C. Unusually for a fruit, they also contain vitamin E and some iron. Another rather unfruit-like property of goji berries is the amount of protein they contain.

Goji berries' high antioxidant content suggests that they might help prevent diseases such as cancer and heart disease. But, as they are so new on the nutritional scene, it's not possible to say yet just how strong their health benefits are. Try them to add some variety to your diet, but don't forget there's no single 'superfood' that can guarantee good health. You still need to ensure you get your minimum five portions of fruit and vegetables a day – and these can come from any fruit and veg, not just the new and exotic ones.

THE MAGNIFICENT 7 – HEART-HEALTHY FOODS

1. Oats
2. Salmon
3. Blueberries
4. Brazil nuts
5. Garlic
6. Green tea
7. Soya milk

'There is a definite link between salt and high blood pressure'

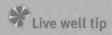
Live well tip
When you're out shopping, read the labels and look for foods with 0.25g salt or less per 100g (0.1g sodium or less per 100g) – this is low (for a manufactured food).

WHAT NOT TO EAT

Saturated and trans fats

Eating saturated and trans fats increases your harmful LDL cholesterol levels and increases your risk of clots, which can cause heart attacks and strokes.

Cut down on your saturated and trans fats by:
- Cutting fast food down or out
- Making as much of your food from scratch as possible
- Replacing most or much of the red meat in your diet with poultry or, even better, beans and lentils
- Switching to low-fat dairy foods

Alcohol

While some studies suggest that a little alcohol (especially red wine) helps to reduce the chance of men, or women past the menopause, having a heart attack or stroke, too much alcohol greatly increases your risk. Drinking more than one or two units of alcohol a day raises your blood pressure, so you're more likely to have a heart attack or stroke.

Salt

There is a definite link between salt and high blood pressure. Since high blood pressure is one of the main contributors to heart attacks and stroke, it makes sense to cut the amount of salt you eat.

We're recommended to eat no more than 6g of salt per day, or 2.5g sodium (which is the harmful component of salt), but less is better. Don't worry about going too low – we only need 1g of salt in our diet, and it's virtually impossible to reduce intake below that if you eat any manufactured foods at all (including staples such as bread).

For more on cutting the salt in your diet, see page 47.

BLOOD PRESSURE

The higher your blood pressure, the more strain is placed on your heart, and the more likely you are to have a heart attack or stroke.

One in four adults in the UK suffer from high blood pressure, but a third of these don't even know it. The only way to find out is to have your blood pressure measured.

Your blood pressure rises gradually as you get older, and you can also inherit a tendency to have high blood pressure. If you are diabetic, your blood pressure is likely to be higher (and your doctor will want to keep a careful eye on this).

Have your blood pressure measured – and ask your doctor for advice if it's high. There's a lot you can do through changing your diet and lifestyle but, if this doesn't work, your doctor may prescribe medication.

Heart-friendly recipes

The following recipes contain nutrients which are particularly useful in promoting a healthy heart.

VEGETABLE BIRIYANI
(Serves 4)

1 tsp sunflower oil
2 medium onions, peeled and chopped
2 cloves garlic, peeled and crushed
2 tbsp medium curry paste
1 small cauliflower cut into florets
2 medium carrots, peeled and diced
1 red pepper, deseeded and diced
100g/4oz green beans, cut in half
1 organic vegetable stock cube
450ml/16 fl oz just boiled water
175g/6oz easy-cook long grain rice
100g/4oz frozen peas, thawed
Chopped fresh coriander, to garnish (optional)

1. Heat the oil in a large non-stick saucepan and fry the onion and garlic over a medium heat for 5 minutes until softened and lightly

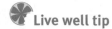

Live well tip
Shed those pounds – If you're overweight, shedding some pounds will reduce the workload of your heart and help keep your blood pressure down.

But there are a lot of factors within your control that can help keep your blood pressure under control and healthy:
● Maintain a healthy weight
● Cut down on the salt in your diet
● Stop smoking
● Reduce the stress in your life
● Take exercise

browned. Stir in the curry paste and cook for 3 minutes. Add all the vegetables except the peas and cook for 1–2 minutes, stirring constantly. Dissolve the stock cube in the just boiled water. Pour the stock over the vegetables and cover the pan.

2. Simmer gently for 20 minutes until the vegetables are tender. Remove the lid and stir in the rice and peas. Replace the lid and simmer gently for a further 20–25 minutes until the rice is cooked and the liquid absorbed.

3. Garnish with fresh coriander and serve with a green salad.

VEGETABLE AND BEAN STEW WITH BASIL OIL
(Serves 4)

1 tbsp olive oil
2 medium onion, peeled and sliced
2 garlic cloves, peeled and crushed
1 medium aubergine, cubed
2 medium courgettes, sliced
1 red pepper, deseeded and diced
1 yellow pepper, deseeded and diced
400g/14oz can chopped tomatoes
2 tbsp tomato puree
410g/14oz can 'no-salt, no-sugar' cannellini beans
2 tsp organic stock powder
1 tsp dried mixed herbs
1 sprig rosemary (optional)
Ground black pepper

For the basil oil:
2 tbsp finely chopped fresh basil
1 tbsp extra virgin olive oil

1. Heat the oil in a large non-stick saucepan and gentle fry the onions and garlic for 3–4 minutes until softened. Add the aubergine, courgettes and peppers and cook for a further 5 minutes until all the vegetables are lightly browned. Stir in the tomatoes, tomato

puree, beans, stock powder, dried herbs and fresh herbs if used. Season with ground black pepper.

2. Place a lid on the pan and simmer for 20–25 minutes until the vegetables are tender.
3. To make the basil oil, mix the chopped basil and the olive oil together in a bowl.
4. Ladle the hot bean stew into deep dishes, top with a little basil oil and serve with warm crusty wholemeal bread or rolls.

Health facts
Extra-virgin olive oil is a rich source of heart-healthy monounsaturated fats, and cannellini beans are a good source of soluble fibre, which helps to lower cholesterol levels.

PESTO CHICKEN WITH FRESH TOMATO SALSA
(Serves 4)

1 large ciabatta
4 small chicken breasts, skinned
2 tbsp red or green pesto sauce, ready made or make your own (see recipes below)
100g/4oz garlic and herb soft cheese
Freshly ground black pepper
1 tsp olive oil

For the salsa:
4 medium tomatoes, peeled, deseeded and sliced
1 small onion, finely chopped
1 clove of garlic, skinned and crushed
A handful of fresh basil (optional)
Freshly ground black pepper.

1. Preheat the oven to 180C/Gas 4.
2. Cut the ciabatta into two vertically and then cut each piece into two horizontally. Cut a deep slit into the side of each chicken breast. Beat together the pesto sauce and soft cheese with a little ground black pepper. Place this mixture in the slits made in the chicken breasts. Brush the chicken breasts with the oil.
3. Bake the chicken breasts for 20–25 minutes or until the chicken is thoroughly cooked.

Health facts
Onions and garlic contain phytochemicals that are good for the heart.

4. Peel the tomatoes for the salsa. Place them in a bowl of boiling water for a few seconds, remove from the water, and you will find that the skins slip off easily.
5. Combine the salsa ingredients in a small bowl.
6. Toast the ciabatta slices and place the cooked chicken breast on the top on to four plates. Place a tablespoon of the salsa by the side and serve with a large salad.

Green pesto

30 fresh basil leaves
1 large sprig of parsley
50g/2oz pine nuts
1 medium garlic cloves
1 tbsp olive oil
2 tbsp freshly grated Parmesan cheese
Freshly ground black pepper
2 tbsp hot water

1. Place the herbs, pine nuts and garlic into a blender and blend until finely chopped. Gradually add the oil and whiz until the mixture forms a thick paste. Add the cheese, pepper and hot water. Whiz for 5 seconds.
2. The pesto can be stored in the fridge, in a screw-top jar, and kept for up to a week.

Red pesto

1 tbsp of oil from the jar of sun-dried tomatoes
Freshly ground black pepper
3 tbsp grated Parmesan cheese
1 tbsp hot water
20 basil leaves
6 sun-dried tomatoes in olive oil
2 medium garlic cloves

1. Put the basil, tomatoes and garlic into a blender and blend until chopped. Add the oil and whiz until the mixture forms a thick paste. Add the pepper, cheese and hot water and blend again for 5 seconds.
2. The pesto can be stored in the fridge, in a screw-top jar, and kept for up to a week.

MUSTARD AND HONEY SALMON (Serves 4)

4 x 175g/7oz fresh salmon steaks, skin removed
3 tsp runny honey
3 tbsp grainy mustard
6 tbsp water
Ground black pepper

1. Place the salmon steaks in a non-stick frying pan (no need to add oil). Cook on a gentle heat for 4 minutes, turn over and continue cooking for 3 minutes until cooked through.
2. Combine the honey, mustard, pepper and water in a small bowl and pour over the salmon. Cook for a further minute. Place a large bed of salad leaves on 4 plates and place a salmon fillet on top. Spoon over the mustard and honey sauce.
3. Serve with boiled new potatoes and broccoli or a green salad.

Health facts
Salmon is a brilliant source of Omega-3 essential fatty acids, which help keep the arteries healthy and prevent heart disease.

QUICK TUNA AND BEAN SALAD (Serves 2)

1 tbsp olive oil
1 tbsp vinegar
Freshly ground black pepper
1 small can sweetcorn, drained
1/2 onion, finely chopped
1 small can kidney beans, rinsed and drained
1 red pepper, deseeded and chopped
1 green pepper, deseeded and chopped
2 tomatoes, cut into wedges
1 large can tuna (in brine), drained and flaked
2 large handfuls of shredded lettuce

1. Combine the olive oil, vinegar, and pepper in a small bowl. Arrange the lettuce on a plate.
2. Put all of the other ingredients, except the tuna and dressing into a bowl and mix together. Add the flaked tuna. Add the oil and vinegar dressing. Combine gently. Spoon the tuna and bean salad over the lettuce leaves. Serve with a warmed crusty wholemeal roll.

Health facts
Although tinned tuna, unlike other oily fish, is not a good source of omega-3s (fresh tuna is better), it is still a good protein source, as are the kidney beans.

LIGHT BANANA AND PECAN PUDDING
(Serves 4)

Sunflower oil for greasing
2 medium eggs, separated
25g/1oz light muscovado sugar
1 medium ripe banana, mashed
40g/1oz shelled pecan nuts, chopped
100g pack ground almonds
Low-fat Greek yoghurt, red berry fruits and maple syrup to serve

1. Preheat the oven to 180C/Gas 4.
2. Grease and line 1.2-litre/2-pint pudding basin with non stick baking parchment.
3. Using an electric whisk, beat the egg yolks and sugar until pale and creamy. Beat in the mashed banana then stir in the nuts and ground almonds. Whisk the egg whites until stiff then gently fold into the egg yolk mixture using a metal spoon. Spoon the mixture into the prepared pudding basin. Take a deep baking tray and quarter fill with water. Stand the pudding basin in the tray. Bake in the oven for 40–45 minutes until the pudding is firm and well risen.
4. When the pudding is cooked, remove from the basin and serve in wedges with fresh berry fruits, maple syrup and Greek yoghurt.

HONEY AND BANANA MUFFINS
(Makes 12)

25g/1 oz soft light brown sugar
200g/8oz white self-raising flour, sifted
50g/2oz wholemeal self raising flour
2 small bananas, mashed
50g/2oz low-fat spread, melted
2 medium eggs
5 tbsp semi-skimmed or skimmed milk
2 tbsp runny honey

Health facts
Pecan nuts and almonds are rich in heart healthy fats and also provide good amounts of calcium and vitamin E. Bananas are great for potassium, which helps regulate blood pressure.

1. Preheat the oven to 200C/Gas 6. Line a bun tray with 12 paper cake cases.
2. Place the sugar, flour, mashed banana and melted butter in a large bowl and mix together. In another bowl mix the eggs, milk and honey and add to the banana mixture. Mix together but do not overbeat. Divide between the 12 cake cases and cook immediately. Bake in the centre of the preheated oven for about 15 minutes until the muffins have risen and are firm.
3. Cool on a wire rack.

FRUIT AND NUT TEABREAD
(Makes 8 slices)

350g/12oz mixed dried fruit
150ml/1/4 pint water
50g/2oz walnuts, chopped
1 large egg
150g/6oz self-raising flour
25g/1oz wholemeal self-raising flour
75g/3oz Demerara sugar
1 large egg
1 tbsp Demerara sugar for topping

1. Preheat the oven to 180C/Gas 4. Line a 450g/1lb loaf tin with non-stick baking parchment.
2. Put the fruit in a saucepan with the water. Bring to the boil. Turn off the heat and allow to stand for 45 minutes. Drain off any remaining water.
3. Place the fruit into a large basin and add the nuts, egg and the sugar. Beat well. Gradually sift in the flour and stir to combine. Spoon into the lined baking tray and sprinkle with the remaining tablespoon of Demerara sugar.
4. Place in the centre of the heated oven for 50 minutes until the teabread has risen and is firm to the touch. (When the bread is cooked, a skewer inserted in the centre should come out clean.) Leave the loaf in the tin for 15 minutes then place on a cooling rack until completely cold. Store in an airtight container.

Health facts
Banana provides sweetness and moistness to these muffins. It's also a good source of potassium.

Health facts
This fruit bread is low in added sugar – the dried fruit provides plenty of natural sugar, along with plenty of fibre. The walnuts are a good source of heart-friendly unsaturated fats.

Eat To Beat – Cancer

Cancer is scary – it's the second most common cause of death in the UK. But there's a lot you can do to reduce your risk:
- Don't smoke, and stay away from smoky places
- Take exercise
- Drink alcohol only in moderation
- Keep your weight under control
- Eat a healthy diet

THE ANTI-CANCER DIET

Poor diet could be a factor in 30 to 40 per cent of cancers, so, by eating healthily, you dramatically increase your chances of staying cancer free.

Fruit and vegetables

These are the top cancer preventers. Fruit and vegetables help protect you against all cancers, and especially those of the digestive system, including mouth, oesophagus, stomach and bowel cancer.

Fruit and veg are packed with antioxidants, such as vitamin C, which neutralise harmful free radical molecules. Along with their other 'crimes', from causing wrinkles to promoting clogged arteries, free radicals can also trigger cancer by damaging the DNA in our cells to cause mutations.

Fruit and vegetables also contain many other exotically named plant chemicals that seem to have anti-cancer properties, including phenols, indoles, flavones and isothiocyanates.

Eat as much fruit and vegetables as you can – go for a brightly coloured mixture to gain the maximum benefit.

- Eat broccoli: the cabbage family – broccoli, cabbage, Brussels sprouts, kale and cauliflower – are particularly cancer-protective: they contain sulforaphane, which boosts immunity and helps prevent cancers forming, isothiocyanates, which make cancer cells 'self-destruct', while indoles reduce the risk of breast cancer.
- Eat tomatoes: for lycopene, a phytochemical found especially in tomatoes, that reduces prostate cancer risk.
- Eat cherries and strawberries: for ellagic acid, which could help inactivate cancer-causing chemicals.
- Eat garlic: along with onions it could help protect against stomach cancer, due to the phytochemical allicin. Onions and garlic are also rich in the antioxidant mineral selenium.

There seems to be more to fruit and vegetables' anti-cancer effects than just antioxidants, and this is why we should concentrate on eating plenty of *real* food rather than popping supplement pills. It seems there's something in food – or perhaps the way different foods work in combination – that just can't be replicated in artificial form.

Fibre

Eating plenty of fibre decreases your risk of many cancers, especially bowel (colon) cancer. A study of thousands of people found those who ate the most fibre were 40 per cent less likely to develop bowel cancer than those who ate the least.

How does fibre work to prevent bowel cancer? It seems that insoluble fibre (from wholegrains, fruit and vegetables) bulks up the contents of your digestive system and smooths it through your bowels, reducing the amount of time that potential carcinogens (cancer-causing chemicals) spend in contact with your bowel walls. Soluble fibre (from oats, pulses, fruit and vegetables) helps to feed 'friendly bacteria' in the bowel that produce chemicals that help prevent tumours from developing.

EAT LESS OF THESE FOODS

Fat and saturated fat

A high-fat diet is linked to an increased risk of colorectal cancer, and too much saturated fat can increase your risk of breast cancer.

What you can do:

- Watch your fat intake, and switch to low-fat cooking methods
- Cut down on high-fat foods such as sausages, burgers and other processed meats
- Try to replace the saturated fat in your diet with healthy unsaturated alternatives, such as olive oil

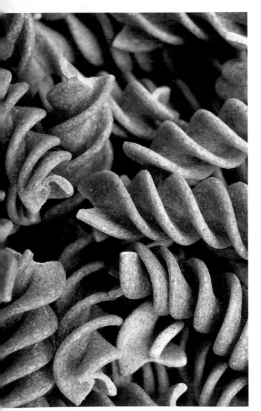

Red meat

A high intake of red meat is linked to an increased risk of bowel cancer, and possibly stomach cancer. Cooking food until it's charred can also produce cancer-causing chemicals.

What you can do:

- Switch from red meat to poultry, fish and pulses – you'll also reduce your heart disease risk
- If you currently eat red meat more than twice a week, cut down to less than once a week and cut your bowel cancer risk by a third

Salt

Too much salty food could increase your risk of stomach cancer. Since it raises blood pressure too, what more reason do you need to cut down?

What you can do:

- Make as much of your food as possible from scratch
- Buy low-salt brands
- Don't add salt at the table

Alcohol

Too much alcohol has been linked with an increased risk of mouth, liver, throat and breast cancer.

What you can do:
- Drink no more than two units a day
- Make at least two or three days each week alcohol-free

10 TOP ANTI-CANCER FOODS
- Tomatoes – rich in lycopene
- Blueberries – full of antioxidant pigments called anthocyanins
- Broccoli – rich in folic acid, the powerful antioxidant betacarotene, as well as cancer-blocking isothiocyanates
- Sweet potatoes – for betacarotene
- Lentils – low-fat and packed with fibre
- Curry spices – including ginger, turmeric, cardamom and chilli, contain powerful antioxidants and salicylic acid
- Tofu – contains the phytochemical genistein
- Brazil nuts – a great source of the antioxidant mineral selenium
- Onions and garlic – good sources of allicin and the antioxidant selenium
- Blackcurrants – excellent for the antioxidant vitamin C

Watch your weight
By maintaining a healthy weight, you'll cut your risk of many cancers, including bowel cancer, and some hormone-dependent cancers such as breast and endometrial cancer.

Recipes that can help prevent cancer

The following recipes all contain nutrients with strong anti-cancer properties.

LENTIL AND SMOKED BACON SOUP
(Serves 4)

3 rashers lean rindless smoked back bacon, fat removed and cut into pieces
1 medium onion, peeled and chopped
1 clove garlic, crushed
3 celery sticks cut into thin slices
4 medium carrots
1 leek, trimmed and cut into slices
2 tsp organic stock powder
1.2 litres/2 pints just-boiled water
200g/8oz split red lentils, rinsed
1 bay leaf
Ground black pepper
Chopped fresh parsley, to garnish (optional)

1. Warm a large non-stick saucepan on the hob and gently fry the bacon for 1 minute. Add the onion, garlic and celery and cook for 3 minutes until beginning to soften. Add the carrots and leek and cook for a further 2–3 minutes, stirring regularly. Stir in the stock powder and the just boiled water and stir thoroughly. Add the lentils and the bay leaf.
2. Bring to the boil. Lower the heat, place a lid on the saucepan and simmer gently for 30–40 minutes until the lentils are tender. Season with black pepper.
3. The soup can be served chunky or allowed to cool for a few minutes and then blended carefully until smooth using a stick blender. Garnish with chopped parsley if used and serve with crusty wholemeal bread or rolls.

BROCCOLI, PEA AND WALNUT TAGLIATELLE
(Serves 4)

300g/12oz tagliatelle (or spaghetti, preferably wholemeal)
200g/8oz broccoli florets
100g/4oz frozen peas, cooked
1 small onion, chopped
2 tbsp olive oil
2 cloves garlic, crushed
100g/4oz walnuts, chopped
1 slice wholemeal bread, crumbed
1/2 tsp chilli flakes
Ground black pepper to serve

1. Cook the tagliatelle according to the packet instructions. Cook the broccoli in boiling water until just tender, adding the peas for the last 2 minutes of cooking time.
2. Heat the oil in a non-stick frying pan and gently fry the onion, garlic, walnuts, chilli flakes and breadcrumbs until the crumbs are crisp. When cooked drain the pasta and peas and broccoli and combine in one saucepan.
3. Place on to four serving plates and scatter over the cooked breadcrumb mixture. Serve with a lettuce and tomato salad.

Health Facts
Broccoli is rich in antioxidant betacarotene, as well as anti-cancer phytochemicals called glucosinolates.

SPANISH PRAWNS AND SPAGHETTI
(Serves 4)

200g/8oz wholemeal spaghetti
6 spring onions or one small onion, finely chopped
1 red pepper, deseeded and finely chopped
1 clove garlic, crushed (optional)
1/4 tsp dried chilli flakes or chilli powder, or to taste
1 tbsp chopped fresh parsley (optional)
1 large tin chopped tomatoes, drained
150g/6oz cooked frozen prawns, defrosted
Ground black pepper to serve

1. Cook the spaghetti according to the packet instructions.
2. Meanwhile, lightly oil a non-stick pan and fry the onions, red pepper, garlic and chilli flakes for 2–3 minutes, stir in the tomato and cook for another 2 minutes. Add the parsley if used and the prawns and cook until the prawns are heated through.
3. Drain the pasta and add to the sauce. Serve immediately with a large mixed salad.

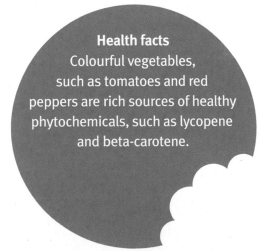

Health facts
Colourful vegetables, such as tomatoes and red peppers are rich sources of healthy phytochemicals, such as lycopene and beta-carotene.

ORANGE AND FIG BAKED APPLES
(Serves 4)

4 large eating apples
4 dried figs, chopped
3 tbsp pistachio nuts, shelled and chopped
Finely grated jest of half an orange
Juice of 1 orange
150ml/5fl oz just-boiled water
1 cinnamon stick, broken in half
0% Greek yoghurt or low-fat fromage frais to serve

1. Preheat the oven to 170C/Gas 3.
2. Keeping the apples whole, remove the core and score the skin around the 'equator' of each apple. Mix the figs, nuts and orange zest together. Stand the apples on an oven-proof dish and fill the centres with the fig and nut mixture. Place the orange juice in a jug and make up to 250ml/8fl oz with just-boiled water. Pour around the apples and add the broken cinnamon stick.
3. Bake in the oven for about 50 minutes until the apples are tender. Serve with spoonful of Greek yoghurt or fromage frais.

Health facts
Apples are a good source of pectin – a type of soluble fibre that can help to reduce high blood cholesterol levels. They also contain potassium.

Eat To Beat – Diabetes

Diabetes occurs when the body is unable to control its blood-sugar levels. Normally after a meal our blood glucose (sugar) rises, and the body secretes the hormone insulin, which removes glucose from the bloodstream and so prevents blood sugar from rising to potentially high levels. But, in diabetics, the control mechanism doesn't work effectively, because no insulin or not enough insulin is produced, or the body doesn't respond to it properly.

The main factors that lead to type-2 diabetes appear to be:
- Being overweight or obese, especially if you're an 'apple-shape' who carries their weight around their middle
- Eating an unhealthy diet
- Not taking enough exercise

In short, the same kind of fat and unfit lifestyle that puts you at risk of many of the other health problems in this book!

The number of people with type-2 diabetes – the commonest form of the disease – is rising alarmingly, and much of this increase can be blamed on our unhealthy diets and lifestyles. Between 1996 and 2004, the number of diagnosed diabetics increased from 1.4 million to 1.8 million, and the figure could hit 3 million by 2010. And this is just the tip of the iceberg – about 50 per cent of diabetics don't know they have the condition. Type-2 diabetes develops gradually – the symptoms are initially minor – and most people have had the condition for several years before they're diagnosed.

Although some of your type-2 diabetes risk is inherited – and you can't do anything to change that – there is a lot you can do to reduce your chances of developing the disease.

Type-2 diabetes used to be called 'adult-onset diabetes' because it was rarely diagnosed in anyone under forty. But now it's being seen in younger and younger people, and even teenagers. Surely this is a wake-up call for us to smarten up our diets and lifestyles?
Some people are more at risk from type-2 diabetes, and you should be especially careful about your diet and lifestyle if you have a family history of diabetes, especially if you are overweight or obese.

Not taking much exercise further increases your risk. Anyone should see their GP if they notice the symptoms of diabetes.

'PRE-DIABETES' – INSULIN RESISTANCE

There's a stage before actual type-2 diabetes where the body is unable to use sugar properly and the sugar levels in the blood rise higher than normal after eating – but not yet high enough to be considered true diabetes.

If caught at this stage, the condition is much easier to deal with – you may be able to control it simply by losing weight, taking more exercise (physical activity helps insulin to work more effectively), and watching what you eat. Over time, however, you may have to take tablets or insulin injections to keep your blood-sugar levels stable.

TIPS TO AVOID TYPE-2 DIABETES

- If you're overweight, get down to a healthy weight
- Eat plenty of fibre – from fruit and vegetables, wholegrains, beans and lentils
- Replace saturated and trans fats in your diet with healthy unsaturated fats
- Make sure you don't eat too much fat of any kind – it can all lead you to pile on the pounds
- Replace red meat with poultry, fish, beans and lentils
- Eat at least five portions of a variety of fruit and vegetables every day
- Increase your physical activity

DIABETES SYMPTOMS

- Being extremely thirsty
- Needing to go to the loo frequently
- Fatigue
- Losing weight, despite being ravenously hungry (more common in type-1 than type-2 diabetes)
- Blurred vision
- Sores that are slow to heal

WHAT ABOUT TYPE-1 DIABETES?

Although both type-1 and type-2 diabetes result in faulty blood-sugar control, they have different causes. Type-1 generally develops in people under thirty, and is thought to be due to their own immune systems attacking the cells that should produce the sugar-control hormone insulin.

DIABETES MYTH BUSTER

Eating too much sugar can't 'give you' diabetes. But it can contribute to you putting on weight, dramatically increasing your diabetes risk.

Exercise For Health

If all of the health benefits of exercise could be bottled, it would be a bestseller at the chemist's and health-food store. But unfortunately they can't – so it's down to us!

It's not enough just to eat well – without exercise you'll never reach your full health potential. Regular physical activity – and this doesn't have to mean hours at the gym – has proven benefits, especially for the heart. But most of us are missing out on all these plus points – only about 40 per cent of men and 30 per cent of women get the recommended amount of physical activity.

Improving your physical fitness brings many important health benefits:
● Strengthens bones, helping to ward off osteoporosis
● Relieves stress and anxiety
● Improves concentration
● Improves posture
● Strengthens the immune system
● Reduces the risk of developing type-2 diabetes
● Boosts metabolism
● Stimulates the body to produce endorphins, natural 'feel-good' chemicals

HOW MUCH EXERCISE?

In 2004 the government's chief medical officer recommended that for general health we should take at least thirty minutes of moderate-intensity physical exercise on five or more days a week. To prevent obesity this should be increased to 45–60 minutes each day. We should also have at least two thirty-minute sessions of resistance exercise twice a week.

It's not difficult to discover why so many of us are less active than earlier generations: our lifestyles have changed dramatically. Many more of us now have jobs that involve sitting all day, working long hours, or commuting by car and public transport. We also rely on labour-saving devices like washing machines and vacuum cleaners, which take the manual effort out of housework.

But there's another reason why many people are put off taking exercise – magazines and television programmes with their pictures of lithe, athletic gym-bunnies and musclemen with sculpted six-packs give the impression that exercise has to be hot, sweaty and strenuous and is something best left to the young and super-fit. But research has shown this is far from the truth. Everyone can achieve health benefits gained from even moderate activity like gardening, housework and walking.

Fact
The American Heart Association attributes 12 per cent of the total deaths in the USA to lack of regular physical activity, and the proportion is likely to be very similar in the UK.

We can all gain by increasing our activity, whatever our present level of fitness. In fact, the lower our level of fitness, the greater the benefits to be gained from exercise. If a couch potato decides to take a fifteen-minute walk it will have more benefit for them than if someone who is already super-fit adds an extra fifteen minutes to their workout.

We all need a combination of three kinds of exercise to maintain fitness:
- Aerobic exercise – the kind of exercise that allows you to run for the bus without getting out of breath
- Resistance exercise – the kind of exercise that enables you to lift heavy weights, from dumbbells to toddlers
- Flexibility exercise – the kind of exercise that enables you to touch your toes with ease

You need them all – it's no good being able to run a marathon if you don't have the strength to lift heavy shopping bags into the car!

We'll explore flexibility in more depth in the next Lifestage, but for now we'll concentrate on the other two kinds of fitness.

Examples of aerobic exercise include:

- Walking (including on a treadmill)
- Jogging
- Cycling
- Rowing (including on a rowing machine)
- Skipping
- Dancing
- Swimming
- Many exercise classes

WARMING UP

Before you start your aerobic exercise, warm up for five to ten minutes. Just do whatever activity you were going to do, but less intensely. This will gradually increase your heart and breathing rate, and warm up your muscles. Cool down with another five to ten minutes of less intense exercise afterwards, to allow your heart rate to return to normal.

AEROBIC EXERCISE

Aerobic exercise is also called cardiovascular exercise or just 'cardio'.

Aerobic exercise:

- Improves the health of your heart and lungs
- Increases stamina
- Helps burn body fat
- Improves circulation
- Helps your cholesterol balance
- Slows down age-related muscle and bone loss

What does it involve?

This is the kind of exercise that gets you out of breath, and your heart pumping. It's good for you because it strengthens the heart muscle, making it more efficient. Even moderate exercise can also boost 'good' HDL cholesterol, aid the circulation of blood around the body and lower blood pressure. All of these reduce your risk of heart attack and stroke. And, if that's not enough to recommend aerobic exercise, it can also help you lose weight and maintain a healthy weight once you've reached your target.

To benefit your heart, exercise needs to be sustained and last at least 15 minutes at a time.

You should be able to carry on a short conversation while doing aerobic exercise – not able to gabble away nineteen to the dozen, but not gasping for breath either!

RESISTANCE (STRENGTH) EXERCISE

Resistance training is also known as strength training or weight training.

Why should you do it?

Resistance training will:
- Increase your muscular strength
- Improve your physique, making you look more lithe and toned
- Improve your endurance
- Boost your metabolism
- Slow age-related muscle and bone loss

Having stronger muscles not only affects the size of the weights you can lift at the gym, but also how far you can kick a football, or hit a shuttlecock, and even how easily you can wield the vacuum cleaner and mow the lawn.

As well as improving endurance and energy, muscle-strengthening exercise also makes you more resistant to injury when you're exerting yourself, and slows the natural muscle and bone loss that occurs as we grow older.

Building muscle also boosts your metabolism, because muscle is an active tissue that burns calories, while fat is metabolically inactive tissue that just sits there and doesn't burn any calories. So, when you build muscle, you're turning yourself into a lean, mean, fat-burning machine!

What is resistance training?

Until fairly recently, resistance training was something reserved for would-be body builders and Olympic weightlifters. Now its importance as part of everyone's fitness regime has been recognised, and we're all being urged to lift those weights.

Resistance training involves progressively 'overloading' your muscles so they gradually get stronger to meet the new challenges you set them. It may sound complicated but all you need is the weight of your own body to get started. Push-ups and sit-ups are just two

WARMING UP

Before a resistance training session, you should warm up with five to ten minutes of low-intensity aerobic exercise – something like brisk walking on a treadmill – to increase your heart rate and blood flow, and warm up your muscles. Cool down with the same afterwards.

examples of resistance exercises that don't require any equipment at all. But you can also use dumbbells, resistance bands or the more complex resistance exercise equipment provided at gyms – they may look like lunar landing craft or medieval instruments of torture, but they are efficient and fun to use.

Resistance training will give you both strength and endurance:
● Strength gains come from how much weight you lift
● Endurance gains come from how many times you lift the weight in succession

If you are a novice at the weights game, you might want to consult a certified professional to devise the correct programme for your fitness level.

Starting with weights

Experts advise that novices should start a weight-training programme using light weights – ones you can lift comfortably eight to twelve times – and a small number of repetitions. Do at least one exercise for each muscle group, moving from the larger muscles (the legs) down to smaller ones (arms).

Check your technique

If you use the wrong technique, you could injure a muscle. Proper technique involves slow, controlled lifts. Slower movements are harder, and provide more benefit. Take three or four seconds for each movement, through the entire range of motion, to provide the most resistance.

Don't hold your breath while you are lifting as this can raise your blood pressure. Breathe normally, breathing out when you are doing the most strenuous part of the exercise.

Allow at least one day between weight-training sessions to let your muscles recover – you'll build strength more quickly this way. Between sessions is the time when your muscles build themselves up, not when you're actually exercising.

The good thing about strength training is that you're likely to see rapid improvements in your muscle tone and strength. But don't be surprised if visible improvements begin to taper off after a few weeks. As your fitness level improves, further improvements take longer to be noticeable. Vary your programme so you don't get bored.

Exercise doesn't have to be actual gym sessions and workouts – there are plenty of other ways to sneak activity into your day.

It doesn't matter what you do to get moving, but it is important to find physical activities that you enjoy and that you can fit in with your daily lifestyle. Start slowly and gradually build up.

Get moving by:
- Taking the stairs instead of the lift
- Riding an exercise bike while you're watching TV
- Going for a brisk fifteen-minute walk during your lunch break
- Walking to the shops, instead of taking the car
- Making a Saturday-morning walk part of your family weekend
- Joining the children for a weekend swim
- Joining in when you take the children for a game of football in the park instead of sitting on the sidelines
- Enrolling in a dance class – there's something to suit everyone
- Buying an exercise or yoga video – and use it, don't just watch it! (You can often borrow them from your local library, so you can ring the changes when you get bored)
- Joining a fitness club – local authorities and schools often have fitness suites, or you could join a private gym
- Trying one of the martial arts
- Getting out your bicycle and helmet and going for a fifteen-minute ride, or using it to get to work

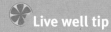 **Live well tip**
It's a habit – according to the University of Pittsburgh, if you do something for just 21 days it becomes a habit. So it won't take you long to make exercise part of your routine.

'When you plan your own "get active" programme, don't set yourself lofty goals that will make you feel guilty or disappointed if you don't reach them'

BE REALISTIC

When you plan your own 'get active' programme, don't set yourself lofty goals that will make you feel guilty or disappointed if you don't reach them. It's far easier to add new activities and targets when you're ready.

If you're going to keep it up, your exercise schedule needs to suit your lifestyle, so, before you get started, decide:

- Where you like to exercise – inside or outside – and find activities to suit
- Whether you prefer to exercise alone or with others – this will help you decide whether you want to attend classes and a gym, or put an exercise video on the TV and lift weights in your bedroom
- What time of day you prefer to exercise – morning, afternoon or evening – but remember that you don't need to do all of your exercise in one go, it can be divided into several shorter sessions
- Whether you would prefer working out with a friend – you will be able to encourage each other and you're both more likely to keep at it
- Whether you might consider hiring a personal trainer to give you advice and keep you motivated, even if it's just for a few sessions

SAFETY FIRST

If you have a health problem (for example you're overweight, or have a heart problem, diabetes or arthritis), if you smoke or if you're in any doubt whether it's safe for you to exercise, you should ask your GP before beginning an exercise programme.

You also shouldn't exercise when you're injured or if you've got a cold or flu. And stop your exercise session immediately if you feel any sudden pain in any part of your body, or if you feel dizzy.

BIG ISSUE – Hormones And Brain Chemicals

Female hormones have a lot to answer for. They can make women's lives miserable through the emotional and physical symptoms of premenstrual syndrome (PMS). And, while many women sail through the menopause with no problems whatsoever, a lot experience symptoms such as hot flushes, mood swings and weight gain, which are hard to deal with.

But help is at hand – we now know that the foods we eat have a large impact on our hormones, and by eating the 'good hormone' foods, and removing the foods that make the problems worse, we can help to keep our hormones in balance and minimise those distressing symptoms.

TACKLING PMS

Up to 90 per cent of women are thought to suffer one or more symptoms before (and sometimes for the first few days of) their period.

Fortunately, women don't have to accept the discomfort as 'part of being female'. Changing the way you eat can help by alleviating the symptoms directly, for example by boosting energy levels, reducing water retention or relieving food cravings. There's also evidence to suggest that certain foods can help to address the root cause, by rebalancing the hormonal imbalances that lie behind PMS.

'Female hormones have a lot to answer for. They can make women's lives miserable through the emotional and physical symptoms of premenstrual syndrome (PMS)'

PMS quiz

Do you experience any of these symptoms in the days before your period?

☐ Do you have cravings for sugar, chocolate and carbohydrate foods?

☐ Do you feel excessively hungry before your period?

☐ Do you suffer from headaches?

☐ Do you have mood swings?

☐ Are you irritable?

☐ Do you feel anxious?

☐ Do you feel insecure?

☐ Are you sometimes tearful?

☐ Do you experience water retention or feel bloated?

☐ Do you have tender or lumpy breasts?

☐ Are you clumsy or forgetful?

☐ Are you tired?

If any of the above symptoms are significantly worse before your period, you could have PMS, which could be helped by following our nutritional advice.

The beat-PMS diet

There's a wealth of nutrients that can lessen PMS symptoms:

● Slow-release carbohydrates: like wholegrains, to relieve energy dips and mood swings

● Phyto-oestrogens: found in soya products such as tofu, miso and tempeh, seeds such as linseeds, and celery – they could help relieve symptoms caused by fluctuating levels of the female hormone oestrogen

● Omega-3 essential fatty acids: from oily fish, flaxseeds and their oil – they appear to relieve some of the physical symptoms of PMS

● Omega-6 essential fatty acids: an omega-6 called GLA, found in evening primrose oil, has produced good results for women suffering from painful or swollen breasts before their periods – ask your doctor or a registered nutritionist or dietician for advice on a supplement

- Calcium and vitamin D: from low-fat dairy products – population studies show that women low in calcium and vitamin D are more likely to have PMS
- Magnesium: from nuts and seeds, pulses and green vegetables – most women with PMS are low in this mineral
- Potassium: from nuts, sesame seeds and bananas, it can help banish bloating
- Water: strange as it sounds, drinking plenty of water also helps to prevent bloating

Bad foods for PMS

Other foods can make your symptoms worse. Try to avoid or reduce these, particularly in the two weeks before your period:

- Caffeine (cut out if possible)
- Salt (cut down)
- Saturated fat (cut down)

THE MENOPAUSE YEARS

Around the age of 40 to 55, most women's levels of the female hormone oestrogen gradually fall, leading to a decrease in fertility, and the changes associated with the menopause.

Symptoms vary, but include:

- Hot flushes
- Night sweats
- Fatigue
- Depression
- Mood swings
- Panic attacks
- Breast pain
- Vaginal dryness
- Sleep disturbance

Many women dread the menopause, but by taking control of your diet, eating the foods shown to relieve your symptoms and cutting out those that trigger them, the whole experience can be a whole lot smoother.

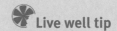
Live well tip

Eat little and often – this will help maintain your energy levels and prevent the mood swings that can go with fluctuating blood sugar. Dried fruit and (unsalted) nuts, or oatcakes spread with a little honey, make excellent snacks.

Live well tip
Learn to de-stress – there
seems to be a link between
relieving stress and an
improvement in PMS
symptoms, so try relaxation
techniques. Exercise can help,
too.

A healthy diet and lifestyle helps women to cope. When your
hormones are in turmoil, your body (and mind) are likely to be feeling
under stress, so it's particularly important to be well nourished. A
balanced diet can help to:
● Balance your hormones
● Maintain your energy levels
● Smooth your moods

The healthy menopause diet
All of the advice for PMS holds true for relieving menopause
symptoms. It stands to reason – oestrogen levels are important in
both (fluctuating in PMS and falling during the menopause). And
both involve physical and psychological symptoms that can be
helped by nutrition.

Keeping up your levels of calcium and vitamin D helps maintain
your bones and prevent osteoporosis, so eat plenty of low-fat dairy
products, oily fish where the bones are eaten (such as salmon and
sardines) and sesame seeds. You can also boost your vitamin D levels
by getting fifteen minutes outside in the sunshine every day.

Oestrogen has a protective effect on the heart – but, after the
menopause, this benefit begins to disappear. Concentrate on heart-
healthy foods, like oily fish, fruit and vegetables, and soluble fibre
from oats and pulses (see page 40). And take a look at soya . . .

Soya – what's all the fuss?
Why do women in Japan suffer so much less from menopausal
symptoms than those in the rest of the world? The answer could be
the amount of soya products they eat.

Soya protein, as well as being a great low-fat protein source (helping
to reduce cholesterol levels and reduce your cardiovascular risk),
could also help smooth your way through the menopause, especially
for those who suffer from hot flushes. Soya is rich in phyto-
oestrogens, plant-based oestrogen mimics that can help top up your
levels if your body isn't producing enough.

There's a lot of interest and research being carried out on phyto-oestrogens and the menopause – we still don't really know quite how effective they are. But it appears that you need to eat a couple of portions of foods rich in these nutrients every day, for three to four months, before seeing an improvement. If you want to give it a try, the best sources of phyto-oestrogens are tofu, soya milk, soya desserts and flaxseeds.

Eating plenty of fibre-rich foods, such as fruit, vegetables, wholegrains, beans and lentils, helps keep your digestive system healthy, reduces your heart attack risk and fills you up, helping to prevent the weight gain that's sometimes associated with the menopause.

If your skin becomes drier after the menopause, it could be worth taking a look at your intake of vitamins A and E, and adding some more oily fish, eggs, nuts and seeds to your diet.

Exercise

Exercise can relieve many menopausal symptoms, and weight-bearing exercise (such as brisk walking and jogging) helps prevent the age-related loss of bone density. Aim for thirty to sixty minutes of moderate exercise, five to six days a week.

FOOD AND MOOD

It's impossible to separate our food and our mood. Firstly, our mood affects the food we choose. We turn to 'comfort foods' when we feel down, and going out for a meal is a classic way to celebrate. When we're happy, we're more likely to stick to our healthy-eating resolutions, but, when we're miserable, it's so much easier to give in to temptation.

And the food we eat has a surprisingly large effect on our moods – by manipulating our blood-sugar levels and our brain chemistry.

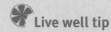 **Live well tip**

Avoid your flush triggers – spicy foods, alcohol, hot soups and hot drinks can trigger hot flushes, so cut them out if they cause you problems.

5 MAGIC MENOPAUSE FOODS

- Mangoes – rich in the antioxidant betacarotene, which the body converts to vitamin A, for smooth skin
- Salmon – high in heart-healthy, mood-smoothing omega-3 essential fatty acids
- Oats – for slow-release carbohydrate, and plenty of sustained energy
- Sesame seeds – rich in calcium and vitamin D for healthy bones, and vitamin E
- Soya products, such as tofu – these could balance your hormones, and are good for your heart

Here are just a few of the main food mood manipulators:

Coffee

Caffeine in coffee and energy drinks (and lesser amounts in tea, cola and chocolate) perks you up and can be a definite mood enhancer. But too much can have the opposite effect, leaving you nervy and anxious – even a single espresso can have this effect if you're particularly sensitive to caffeine.

Chocolate

Chocolate contains caffeine, as well as a caffeine relative called theobromine.

Some scientists say that 'real' chocolate containing 70 per cent cocoa solids or more (not the chocolate typically found in most popular chocolate bars) might affect our mood by working on our neurotransmitters – the brain's chemical messengers that transport electrical signals between nerve cells. It's these signals that cause the changes in our emotions and sensations.

Chocolate also contains a neurotransmitter called anandamide, which acts on the same part of the brain as the active ingredient in cannabis!

But you'd need to eat huge amounts of chocolate in order to get the amount of anandamide you'd expect to need for a mood-boosting effect. And the 'happy chemicals' found in chocolate are in many other foods, so why does chocolate seem to have such mood-raising effects in some people?

Probably most important are the deep-rooted feel-good associations we have with chocolate. Anything we think of as a 'treat' – whether it's food, shopping or simply cuddling the cat – boosts our production of 'feel-good' brain chemicals called beta-endorphins. This could well be the main reason for chocolate's mood-enhancing effect.

Moody minerals and vitamins

Low levels of certain micro-nutrients are associated with an increased susceptibility to depression and low moods, so it makes sense to ensure you eat a healthy, wholefood diet, which will contain plenty of the following:

- Selenium foods: Brazil nuts, sesame seeds, lean meat, fish
- Magnesium foods: Lean meat, low-fat dairy products, green vegetables, nuts and seeds, pulses, wholegrains, dried fruits, mushrooms
- Folic acid foods: Liver, eggs, green leafy vegetables, fortified breakfast cereals, beans and lentils, nuts, citrus fruit, apricots, broccoli, brown rice, wheatgerm

Sugary foods

Grabbing a sugary snack when you're feeling low might seem the perfect solution but, after that fleeting sugar buzz passes, you're actually setting yourself up for a slump.

Sugary foods produce short-lived energy, which leaves you hungry, often anxious and crabby . . . and desperate for another chocolate bar or biscuit!

If you want your moods to remain calm and stable, rather than lurching from sugar-high to sugar-low, what you really need is quality fuel. And, once again, it's those slow-release complex wholegrain starchy carbohydrates, and beans and lentils. Rather than a chocolate muffin, grab a wholemeal bagel with some low-fat cream cheese. Not only will it sustain you for longer than the muffin, it's also lower in fat and calories and higher in vitamins and minerals.

Live well tip

Cut out the crutches – don't rely on alcohol or cigarettes to make you feel better. Alcohol may make you feel 'merry' initially, but it is actually a depressant – hardly what your body needs. And cigarettes – aside from all their other health dangers – are a stimulant that can make you jittery and disrupt your blood-sugar levels.

'Grabbing a sugary snack when you're feeling low might seem the perfect solution, but after that fleeting sugar buzz passes, you're actually setting yourself up for a slump'

Oily fish
Fish could help prevent depression!

Population studies have shown that in countries where a lot of oily fish – the main source of omega-3 essential fatty acids – is eaten, the rate of depression is particularly low, and people with low blood levels of omega-3s tend to have a more negative outlook.

High doses of omega-3s have produced encouraging results in medical trials, by improving people's depression symptoms.

The evidence certainly suggests that omega-3s are somehow involved in feeling happy, so why not boost your intake of these beneficial fats, found mainly in oily fish, but also in flaxseeds and flaxseed oil?

Think about . . .

Even if you're still under fifty and in the second Lifestage, you should be thinking ahead, and considering how the food you eat affects:

- Your stress levels (see page 104) – does your healthy diet slip when the going gets tough?
- Immunity (see page 78) – do you pack your meals with antioxidants?
- Your joints (see page 188) – are you eating enough essential fatty acids?
- Your digestion (see page 212) – do you eat sufficient fibre? How's your fruit and veg intake?
- Osteoporosis (see page 191) – do you combine a bone-healthy diet with plenty of weight-bearing exercise?
- Mental slow-down (see page 198) – is your diet too high in saturated fats and too low in their unsaturated cousins?

Life Stage 3

you are™
what
you eat

Live Well, Live Longer

We all know lithe octogenarians who like nothing better than pulling on their walking boots and tramping in the countryside or donning their dancing shoes for an evening on the dance floor. But they didn't get that way by accident. They didn't drink from some elusive fountain of youth. The chances are they simply learned the secrets of living well to live longer.

HEALTHY EATING FOR THE OVER-FIFTIES

Living younger longer is all about a healthy diet, keeping body and mind active and maintaining our social networks. And, naturally, our genes play a part.

As we age, keeping moving, getting enough rest and relaxation, and making sure our diets contain all the nutrients our bodies need is just as important as at other stages of our lives. Particular anti-ageing nutrients like antioxidants become particularly important.

So what do you need to live longer?

A HEALTHY IMMUNE SYSTEM

Your immune system is like a private army, fighting off the daily invasion of bugs and germs. If it's weakened, invaders may go undetected and be able to multiply. Your immune system works best when it is kept well supplied with a full range of nutrients, is not challenged by pollutants such as cigarette smoke, and when you're not stressed.

A DIET RICH IN ANTIOXIDANTS FOUND IN FRESH FRUIT AND VEGETABLES

Antioxidants are our defence against so-called oxidative damage, which is caused by harmful molecules called free radicals. We can't avoid free radicals – they're produced naturally in the course of everyday life – though factors such as cigarette smoke, pollution, burned or charred food and excessive sun exposure adds to our free-radical load. The free radicals damage body cells – they are implicated in a whole host of health problems, from heart disease and stroke to cancer. They're even involved in ageing and wrinkles!

Antioxidants mop up these free radicals before they can harm us, and the easiest way to get antioxidants is to eat more fruit and vegetables – the fresher the better. Some antioxidants work even better when they're cooked, the lycopene found in tomatoes being an excellent example.

DRINK UP – THE FOUNTAIN OF YOUTH

Tea

Tea is packed with antioxidant plant chemicals called catechins, which are known to lower blood pressure, as well as help to fight heart disease, cancer and osteoporosis. Tea may also protect joints by blocking an enzyme that destroys cartilage, and could help you to lose weight by speeding up your metabolism.

And, if those aren't enough reasons to put the kettle on, tea also helps prevent wrinkles by fighting DNA damage from ultraviolet light, the source not only of skin ageing but also of skin cancer. This is the reason why extract of green tea is often to be found in anti-ageing skin products.

All kinds of tea – including black tea, green tea, white tea, rooibos (redbush) tea and jasmine tea – are rich in catechins and flavonoids, but green tea and white tea contain substantially more than the other kinds. Herb teas and fruit teas, however, don't have the special benefits of the teas above, though they are often high in their own antioxidants.

Wine
Wine has been prized since ancient times for its medicinal properties, but it is only in recent years that many of these have been identified.

A *little* alcohol appears to be beneficial to cardiovascular health. And red wine is particularly good, since red grape skins contains resveretrol – another antioxidant ally in the battle against free radicals – which scientists now believe may also fight the actual ageing process.

In low to moderate amounts – no more than two small glasses a day, preferably with meals – wine can help raise the levels of 'good' HDL cholesterol, protect against heart disease and cancer and lower the risk of Alzheimer's disease.

But remember there are some people on certain medications who should not drink alcohol at all. Always check with your doctor.

THE ULTIMATE ANTI-AGEING DIET

There's no need to make major changes to our diet as we grow older. All we need to do is carry on putting into practice all the advice in this book. But take a look at your portion sizes – our metabolisms slow as we age and it's easy for the pounds to creep on. Blood pressure rises as we age, so it's also important to keep your salt intake low, to help keep it under control.

Much has been written about the anti-ageing properties of the Mediterranean, Japanese and vegetarian diets, and population studies have shown that people eating these diets tend to live longer. So why not give them a try, or at least adopt some of their elements?

If you fancy giving your diet a touch of the Mediterranean sunshine, remember to go easy on the creamy sauces and the cheese and keep an eye on portion sizes – it's all too easy to overdo the pasta. Concentrate on plenty of fresh tomato-based dishes with loads of vegetables and fruit-based desserts.

If you want to try a Japanese diet, watch the salty soy sauce and avoid tempura and other deep-fried dishes when you're preparing dishes at home or eating out.

And adopting some of the elements of a *good* vegetarian diet certainly makes sense. But remember there is such a thing as a *bad* vegetarian diet – cheese-loaded pizza and chips are vegetarian, but eaten regularly wouldn't constitute a healthy diet. If you want to give vegetarianism a try, make sure you are eating a balanced diet so you get all the vitamins and minerals you need. It's easy to miss out on nutrients found mainly, or only, in meat or animal products.

THE MEDITERRANEAN DIET

At first glance the Mediterranean diet may not look particularly healthy. People in Mediterranean countries seem to eat as much fat (sometimes more) than the average person in Britain (30 to 40 per cent of the calories in the traditional Mediterranean diet come from fat). They enjoy meat, creamy sauces and wine.

So what are their health secrets?
- The traditional Mediterranean housewife produces almost all of her family's food from scratch using fresh in-season produce
- Instead of saturated animal fats such as butter or polyunsaturated fats like corn oil or safflower, the Mediterranean choice is almost exclusively monounsaturated olive oil
- They rely very little on processed food and ready-meals, which are often high in sugar, saturated fat and salt
- The Mediterranean diet is rich in cereals, beans, fresh fruits and a variety of vegetables – peppers, aubergines, courgettes, tomatoes, onions and greens

- A wide variety of herbs and spices, including rosemary, thyme, sage and cumin are essential in the cuisine, and many of these contain powerful antioxidants
- Meat, particularly red meat, is used sparingly and in combination with large quantities of vegetables
- Fresh fish (often rich in omega-3s) is served frequently, and generally baked, grilled, steamed or poached rather than deep-fried
- Creamy sauces are part of the cuisine, but they are served only very occasionally
- The Mediterranean people enjoy their cheese but tend to use strong cheeses, so they only need small amounts to flavour dishes – if they have a piece of cheese after a meal it will be a sliver of a strong cheese with a piece of fruit and not a tower of biscuits, lashings of butter and a large hunk of milder cheese
- Desserts other than fruit are reserved for special occasions
- The delicious cakes and pastries available in Spain and Italy are not part of the everyday diet, but just for the occasional treat
- Meals are washed down with a glass of red wine, known to reduce cholesterol levels
- The people have a relaxed attitude and don't hurry their meals

THE JAPANESE DIET

The Japanese diet is considered one of the healthiest national diets, and it's becoming increasingly popular in the West. The Japanese, and the people of Okinawa in particular, are remarkable for their longevity.

This could be because:
- The Japanese diet is high in vegetables
- The Japanese diet is rich in fish, especially those high in omega-3 essential fatty acids, such as salmon and fresh tuna
- Japanese housewives use a lot of soya products in the meals they prepare

- Chicken and meat are used sparingly
- Some kinds of mushrooms used in Japanese cookery – the reishi and shiitake – may protect against heart disease and help to lower cholesterol
- Seaweed, a common component of sushi and other Japanese dishes, is a rich source of B-vitamins as well as vitamin C, vitamin E and iodine, needed for the thyroid gland
- The traditional Japanese drink is green tea, well known for its health-giving properties

SENSATIONAL SOYA

Known as the 'cow of China' and 'meat without bones', soya is an amazing health food, reputed to have immune-boosting, cancer-fighting and heart-healthy properties. In Oriental medicine, soya beans are valued as the tonic for long life and healthy living.

It was studying the health of high-soy-consuming cultures like the Japanese and the Chinese that first alerted scientists to its health-building properties.

The average Japanese person eats 50–75g of soya foods and soya milk every day, whereas in America and the West the average is a meagre 5g, mostly in the form of oil.

When scientists considered differences in the health of Japanese people and those living in the West, they found that the Japanese enjoyed a longer lifespan, had lower rates of cancer and a much lower incidence of heart disease. Some doctors believe that adding 50g of soya to our daily diets could lower the risk of these diseases.

THE VEGETARIAN DIET

A good vegetarian diet is basically a very healthy diet. Population studies have found that vegetarians tend to have lower blood pressure and cholesterol, less heart disease, less type-2 diabetes and less cancer. They're also less likely to be overweight. Note, though, we said 'good' vegetarian diet. If you live on pizza, chips, creamy pasta sauces and full-fat cappuccinos, while neglecting your protein, fruit and vegetables, your nutrient intake – and hence your health – will soon suffer.

These are the features of a good vegetarian diet:
- High in fruit and vegetables
- High in fibre from beans, lentils, wholegrains, starchy carbohydrates and fruit and vegetables (animal products contain little or no fibre or complex carbohydrate)
- Generally low in fat – vegetarians tend to eat up to 25 per cent less fat each day than omnivores
- Vegetarians tend not to eat so much saturated fat, because meat is not included in the diet (however, they must be careful not to eat too much high-fat dairy products, such as full-fat milk and high-fat cheeses, as these also contain saturated fat)

What about deficiencies?

Some people worry that, because it cuts out meat products, a vegetarian diet will leave them short of nutrients, such as protein, iron, zinc and vitamin B12.

Vegetarians can get plenty of protein from pulses, soya products, nuts, seeds and low-fat dairy products. Even without meat, they can get enough iron from dried fruit, molasses, pulses, egg yolks, wholegrains and green vegetables, particularly if they eat foods rich in vitamin C at the same time, to boost their iron absorption. Zinc is found in cheese, nuts and seeds (especially pumpkin seeds), pulses, and tofu. And if they eat dairy products and eggs, vegetarians will probably get plenty of vitamin B12.

The Vegetarian Society recommends a daily diet of:
- 3 or 4 servings of cereals/grains or potatoes
- 4 or 5 servings of fruit and vegetables
- 2 or 3 servings of pulses, nuts and seeds
- 2 servings of milk, cheese, eggs or soya products
- A small amount of vegetable oil and margarine or butter
- Some yeast extract such as Marmite, fortified with vitamin B12

Vegans

Vegans eat no products derived from animals whatsoever – that means no eggs, dairy products or honey.

This means they may be more at risk of deficiencies in vitamin D and vitamin B12. Aside from the vitamin D produced naturally by the action of sunlight on skin and B12 produced in small quantities by 'friendly bacteria' in the gut, these micronutrients are found only in animal products – all off limits for vegans. Vegans and other people who eat and drink no or few dairy products will need to get vitamin B12 from fortified foods such as some soya milks, low-salt yeast extract and fortified breakfast cereals.

Calcium may be a problem for anyone who doesn't consume dairy products, because the calcium contained in most vegan sources is hard for the body to absorb. The best vegan sources are tofu, green leafy vegetables, watercress, dried fruit, seeds and nuts. White bread is fortified with calcium, as are some soya milks.

The science behind the statistics

Lower rates of cardiovascular disease – vegetarians tend to have lower levels of the 'bad' LDL cholesterol, which reduces their risk of clogged arteries. This is probably due to their low intakes of saturated fats, compared to the healthier unsaturated fats.

Lower blood pressure – it's not certain why vegetarians tend to have lower blood pressure. Being more likely to be a healthy weight certainly helps, and the good intake of potassium from plenty of fruit and vegetables could play a part, too.

Type-2 diabetes – vegetarian diets tend to be high in starchy carbohydrates and fibre, which helps keep blood-sugar levels under control. The fact that vegetarians are less likely to be overweight would also contribute to their reduced incidence of diabetes. A good vegetarian diet is very close to the British Diabetic Association's recommendation for diabetic patients, and for diabetes prevention.

Cancer – the World Cancer Research Fund's dietary advice to minimise cancer risk is to cut down on fat and eat more fruits, vegetables and wholegrains, and this fits in very well with a good vegetarian diet. Vegetarianism appears particularly effective at reducing the risk of colon and breast cancer.

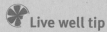 **Live well tip**

Try demi-veg – even if you don't want to commit to total vegetarianism, your body will thank you if you increase the amount of beans and other pulses, fruit, vegetables and wholegrains in your diet, especially if you also decrease your intake of red meat.

AGEING AND WEIGHT GAIN

Have you ever wondered why many people seem to run to 'middle-age spread' as they grow older?

As we age, we lose muscle and bone mass, and as these are the densest substances in the body, you'd expect us to lose weight.

But at the same time, as we grow older and lose all that active, calorie-burning muscle, our basal metabolic rate – the amount of calories we use just for 'ticking over' – decreases. This means we don't need so many calories so, if we eat the same amount of calories and don't burn them off with exercise, we'll store them as fat, leading to an expanding waistline. As they grow older, most people put on 2–4kg (4–8lb) per decade.

Nutrition and exercise is the key to preventing weight gain, and staying strong and healthy.

Eat the right amount of calories:
If eating what you did a few years ago causes you to put on weight, you may need to trim your portion sizes. Just make sure you're still eating a balanced diet, with a good balance of low-fat protein, wholegrains and pulses, and a moderate amount of healthy unsaturated fats, while you minimise your saturated fats. And don't forget to keep up your intake of plenty of fruit and vegetables.

Keep up the exercise:
Keep your metabolism revved up by maintaining your muscle mass. As we age, we lose muscle, but we can slow (or even reverse) the decline with resistance exercise (see page 164). This is because, when we lose muscle, our metabolism slows, and we don't need so many calories. By maintaining or building muscle, you keep your metabolism speedy.

'If eating what you did a few years ago causes you to put on weight, you may need to trim your portion sizes'

Eat To Beat – Arthritis And Other Joint Problems

Arthritis means 'inflamed joints', and the most common form is osteoarthritis. It's rare before the age of 40 but increases with age – most people with osteoarthritis are over 65. Injuries earlier in life (such as sports injuries) also increase your risk.

As wear and tear on the joints accumulates, the layer of cartilage protecting the bone becomes roughened and wears away. The body tries to compensate for the cartilage loss by attempting to repair the damage, creating thickening and outgrowths of the joints, making movement difficult. Meanwhile, the membranes lining the joints can become inflamed.

THE ANTI-ARTHRITIS DIET AND SUPPLEMENTS

More and more evidence is emerging that diet can help prevent and relieve the symptoms of arthritis and painful joints.

Watch your weight

If you're overweight, lose some – carrying too much weight puts strain on your joints, and increases wear and tear. This increases your risk of osteoarthritis, and speeds its progression if it does develop.

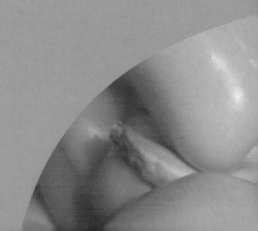

Omega-3s

Omega-3 essential fatty acids (from oily fish and flaxseeds) are involved in maintaining healthy joints, and getting plenty of omega-3s can delay or prevent the development of osteoarthritis.

Recent research has shown that omega-3 supplements can relieve the pain, stiffness and inflammation of arthritis. However, a high dose is generally needed to treat symptoms, so you should consult your doctor, a dietician or a registered nutritionist for advice before trying this. Three to six months' treatment is generally needed to see an improvement.

Evening primrose oil

Evening primrose oil contains an essential fatty acid called GLA, which helps relieve inflammation, and many people swear by it to relieve arthritis. Once again, consult your doctor, dietician or registered nutritionist for advice on how much you'd require. You need to take GLA for up to six months before you could expect any improvement.

Glucosamine

Glucosamine is an amino acid needed to form and rebuild cartilage, and taking glucosamine supplements seems to help ease the pain and stiffness for some people with osteoarthritis. Once again, it's not a quick fix – it takes about two months for it to have an effect, and, if it hasn't done anything by then, it probably won't work for you. Glucosamine is often taken in combination with chondroitin, with or without omega-3s.

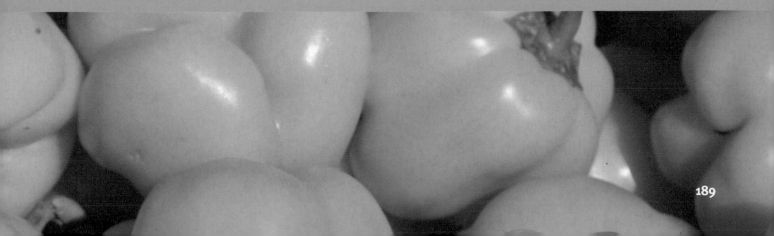

Chondroitin sulphate

Chondroitin sulphate makes up part of your joints' protective cartilage coating, and helps make it stretchy and resilient. There's some evidence that chondroitin supplements can slow the progression of osteoarthritis, so talk to your doctor if you think it might help you. Once again, it takes a few months to act, and doesn't work for everyone.

'If you're being treated for any medical condition, particularly if you're taking medication, you should always talk to your doctor before taking any nutritional supplements'

Eat To Beat – Osteoporosis

Osteoporosis is a condition where your bones become brittle, so they can fracture after even a small impact.

The problem with osteoporosis is that you can't feel your bones thinning – it's sometimes called 'the silent disease'. Often the first symptom is a loss of height (as your weakened spine begins to bow under your own weight), or a bone breaking after a minor bump.

Bone is a dynamic tissue, constantly being broken down and rebuilt. Up until the age of about 35, the pace of bone building outstrips bone breakdown, so your bones grow and become denser. For some years after this, bone is made at about the same rate as it's broken down, so your bone density stays about the same. But, as you age further, the balance tips in favour of bone breakdown, so your bones become thinner and more vulnerable.

When women reach the menopause, their rate of bone thinning accelerates, which is why elderly women are at particular risk from osteoporosis.

Osteoporosis risk factors:
- Family history of osteoporosis
- In women, lack of the female hormone oestrogen, both after the menopause and, in younger women, if their periods have stopped for over six months (aside from pregnancy), for example due to weight and body-fat loss caused by an eating disorder
- In men, lack of the male hormone testosterone
- Long-term use of high-dose steroid drugs (e.g. for asthma medication)
- Lack of activity
- Smoking
- Heavy drinking

You can't change your genes, your age or sex, but there's a lot you can do to boost your bones with diet and exercise.

The sooner you start eating for your bones, the better. Since most bone is built up when you're young, you should try to make as many deposits into your 'bone bank' while your skeleton is still building itself up. Most of our peak bone mass is acquired during adolescence, but the average teenager's calcium intake is 20 per cent lower than recommended.

But you can still help your bones at any age – even if you already have osteoporosis, you can slow the further thinning of your bones by following a bone-friendly diet and taking appropriate exercise. Your doctor may also prescribe supplements and medication.

Older people are less efficient at absorbing calcium from their diets. If you think you may be at risk from osteoporosis, ask your doctor about calcium and vitamin D supplements.

BONE RISK QUIZ

1. Have you ever broken a bone after a minor knock?
2. Are you female?
3. If you're female, have you passed the menopause?
4. Do you have a family history of osteoporosis (sibling, parent or grandparent) or broken hips?
5. Do you diet to lose weight for much of the time?
6. Do you do weight-bearing activities (running, walking, weight training) less than three times a week?
7. Do you get less than fifteen minutes of sun exposure (without sunscreen) every day during the sunny months?
8. Do you eat less than three servings of calcium-rich foods every day? (One serving equals one cup of milk, yoghurt, 1oz of Cheddar cheese, or a serving of tinned salmon or sardines where the bones are eaten)

The more your 'yes' answers, the more your bones are at risk – follow our diet and lifestyle advice to protect them.

THE BONE-FRIENDLY DIET

Strong bones depend on several important nutrients.

Calcium

Low-fat dairy products are an excellent (and probably the best) source of calcium but, if you can't tolerate dairy, there are alternatives.

Good sources:
- If you drink soya milk instead of cow's milk, look for one that's enriched with calcium
- Tofu
- Tinned fish where the bones are eaten (salmon, sardines)
- Seeds, especially sesame seeds
- Dried fruit, especially figs
- Green leafy vegetables
- White bread and white flour (which has to be fortified with calcium by law)

For more on calcium, including 'calcium enemies' that block your absorption of this vital mineral, see page 123.

Vitamin D

The body needs vitamin D in order to absorb calcium and incorporate it into the skeleton.

Good sources: Although the body can produce and store some of its own vitamin D from the effect of sunlight on the skin during the summer months, it's thought that some people – especially if they're elderly and don't get outdoors much, or cover up when they do go out – don't get enough vitamin D from this source. This makes it particularly important for them to top up with dietary vitamin D, from oily fish, eggs, dairy products and spreads enriched with vitamin D. If you're at particular risk of deficiency, especially if your osteoporosis risk is high, your doctor may prescribe a supplement.

'Low-fat dairy products are an excellent (probably the best) source of calcium'

Magnesium

The body uses magnesium when it manufactures vitamin D, and magnesium can help slow bone breakdown.

Good sources: Green vegetables, nuts, low-fat dairy products.

Potassium

Potassium can reduce the rate of calcium loss from the body.

Good sources: Bananas, melon, fish.

Boron

Boron is another mineral involved in vitamin D manufacture by the body, and the absorption of calcium from food.

Good sources: Apples, pears, grapes, nuts, leafy vegetables.

Vitamin K

Vitamin K is used to make osteocalcin, a bone-hardening protein. Vitamin K is also needed to enable fractures to heal.

Good sources: Broccoli, cauliflower, dark-green leafy vegetables.

Phyto-oestrogens

Population studies in countries in Southeast Asia, where a lot of soya products are eaten, have found low rates of osteoporosis (as well as breast cancer and heart disease). Can soya take the credit?

Plant oestrogens called isoflavones are found mainly in soya beans and soya products, but also in chickpeas and other pulses. They are thought to have an oestrogen-like effect on the body, which might suggest that they would help prevent osteoporosis.

But clinical studies to test whether soya, and isoflavone supplements, actually work to prevent osteoporosis have produced conflicting results. The current advice is not to recommend supplements, but to eat moderate amounts of soya products as

Live well tip
Watch what you drink –
excessive caffeine intake (from
drinks like coffee and cola)
can cause excess excretion of
calcium from the body, and
the phosphoric acid in many
fizzy drinks can hinder calcium
uptake from food. Excessive
alcohol is also bad for your
bones – don't drink more than
21 units per week for women
and 28 for men.

part of a balanced diet. Tofu is a very bone-friendly food anyhow –
100g/4oz contains 500mg of calcium, as much as two-thirds of a pint
(380ml) of semi-skimmed milk.

DON'T 'WEIGHT' FOR EXERCISE

Activity is important for maintaining strong bones. Any weight-bearing exercise (one that puts weight on your bones) helps to maintain a strong skeleton. It needn't be high-impact, and 20 minutes a day is enough.

Brisk walking is brilliant, particularly because almost everyone can do it. Other good examples are jogging, stair climbing, running, skipping, tennis, weight training and some yoga and Pilates exercises, such as those where you're balancing on one leg, balancing on all fours, or raising and lowering your legs. If you have been diagnosed with osteoporosis, you should check with your doctor or specialist before trying a new form of exercise, to prevent you from attempting any moves that might put too much stress on your weakened bones.

BONING UP ON A HEALTHY DIET

Try these quick fixes to get more calcium and other bone-friendly nutrients into your diet:

- Have tinned sardines or pilchards on toast with a salad as a light meal
- Try a baked potato topped with a small tin of salmon mashed with plain yoghurt and chives
- Make yoghurt-based salad dressings
- Drink a glass of semi-skimmed milk with your meal
- Replace snacks of crisps and chocolate with dried fruit and nuts
- Baked beans (reduced-sugar, reduced-salt) on toast provides calcium from both beans and bread
- Add semi-skimmed or skimmed milk to soups to increase their calcium content
- Accompany Indian dishes with a raita made from low-fat natural yoghurt, finely chopped cucumber and chopped mint

- Have low-fat rice pudding for dessert – make it yourself (with brown pudding rice and low-fat milk, and only a little sugar) and it'll be even healthier
- Try frozen yoghurt instead of ice cream – it's still high in calcium, and lower in fat

Recipes for healthy bones

The following recipes all contain nutrients which promote bone health.

SPICY PAN-COOKED FISH
(Serves 4)

1 large tin chopped tomatoes
4 tbsp flat leaved parsley, chopped
1/2 tsp chilli powder
Ground black pepper
4 white fish fillets (175g/7oz approx), skin removed (cod, haddock, coley, hoki)
4 tbsp natural low-fat natural yoghurt

1. Place the chopped tomatoes into a large saucepan or lidded frying pan. Add 2 tbsp of the parsley and the chilli powder. Bring to the boil, season with black pepper.
2. Lay the fish on top of the tomato mixture and spoon over a little of the mixture. Place the lid on the pan and gently simmer until the fish is cooked. This will take 5–8 minutes depending on the thickness of the fillets. Stir the yoghurt into the sauce.
3. Serve on a bed of brown rice, with the remaining parsley sprinkled over, with green beans or broccoli.

Health fact
White fish is extremely low in fat and calories, great if you're watching your weight. If you add the yogurt, you'll also be boosting your calcium intake and benefiting your bones.

POACHED FRUIT COMPOTE WITH YOGHURT AND SEEDS
(Serves 4)

50g/2oz dried apricots
75g/3oz dried apricots
100g/4oz dried peaches
100g/4oz stoned prunes
1 litre bottle pressed apple juice
2 wide strips of orange peel
1 cinnamon stick, broken in half
5 cardamom pods, lightly crushed (optional)
2 tbsp pumpkin seeds
2 tbsp sunflower seeds
200ml/8oz pot low-fat Greek yoghurt or virtually fat-free fromage frais

1. Soak the fruit in some of the apple juice for 6 hours or overnight. Place the soaked fruit in a saucepan with the apple juice it was soaked in. Add more apple juice to cover the fruit. Add the orange peel, cardomom pods and cinnamon sticks.
2. Bring to the boil, reduce heat and simmer for 20 minutes until the fruit is tender. Serve hot or cold with Greek yoghurt or fromage frais.
3. Sprinkle the pumpkin and sunflower seeds on the top.

TIP:
Use dried fruit not no-need-to soak fruit for this recipe and buy organic where you can.

Health fact
Yoghurt and fromage frais are good sources of bone-strengthening calcium, which may also help with weight control and reducing high blood pressure.

Eat To Beat – Mental Slowdown

As we grow older, our bodies naturally slow down, and we're unable to do some of the things we did when we were younger. Of course, there's a lot we can do to hold back this natural ageing – as the advice in this book explains – but it's extremely unlikely for an eighty-year-old to feel as strong or as fit as she did at eighteen.

But is it inevitable for your brain to slow down as well? There are plenty of centenarians out there who are sharp as a pin! What's their secret?

A significant amount of the way the brain ages is down to your genes. But a healthy diet, rich in 'brain-friendly' food, can go a long way towards keeping those little grey cells firing on all cylinders. A healthy diet and lifestyle can even reduce the risk of dementias, such as Alzheimer's.

WHAT DOES THE BRAIN NEED?

Diet-wise, it's safe to say that, if it's good for your heart, it's good for your brain, too. Probably the best thing you can do for your brain is keep your arteries in good shape, so all the advice in Eat to Beat Cardiovascular Disease (see page 138) on eating for your heart, and keeping your cholesterol levels healthy, will benefit your brain as well.

When you eat that deep-filled cheese and salami pizza, and all that saturated fat raises your cholesterol and clogs the arteries leading to your heart, it also furs up the arteries in the brain. The brain depends on a healthy blood supply to provide it with oxygen and nutrients. More dramatically, a clogged or damaged artery in the brain can lead to a stroke.

BRAIN-FRIENDLY FOODS

Oily fish

Is there no end to their talents? Once again, oily fish, like salmon, mackerel, trout, sardines, pilchards and fresh tuna, have proven benefits for your health, thanks to their artery-smoothing effects. Studies of elderly people found that those eating oily fish at least once a week were up to 60 per cent less likely to develop Alzheimer's. Try to eat two servings a week.

Green and white tea

Research has shown that Japanese people who drank more than two cups of green tea a day had a 50 per cent lower chance of mental decline than those who drank less green tea. It's the high catechin content in the tea that's thought to provide the benefit. White tea (a special variety, not ordinary tea with milk) is even more catechin-rich than green. White tea wasn't tested in the Japanese study, but it would certainly be worth giving it a try.

Drink your juice

Concord grape juice contains polyphenols (similar to those in tea), which also appear to help slow brain ageing. And new research suggests that apple juice (and apples) could have a similar effect.

Fruit and vegetables

Fruit and vegetables, packed with all those lovely antioxidants, have definite brain benefits, by scavenging the harmful free radicals that damage our bodies' cells – those cells in the artery walls and the brain itself are the ones we're most interested in when trying to keep our brains 'young'. The potassium content in fruit and vegetables helps to control our blood pressure, and they're also rich in folic acid, which is thought to help reduce the risk of mental decline. And – provided you don't smother your fruit in sugar, custard, cream or pastry, drown your vegetables in creamy sauces or eat them all in 'chip form' – they're low in calories, so they help you keep your weight down. Since being overweight has a knock-on harmful effect on your blood pressure and cholesterol levels, that's another brain-friendly plus point for the fruit and veg.

Eat as many portions as you can – and in plenty of colours, to get the maximum variety of antioxidants and phytochemicals.

Healthy oils
Monounsaturated fats, such as those found in olive oil, and nuts and seeds, help lower your 'bad' LDL cholesterol levels and raise your levels of 'good' HDL cholesterol, protecting your arteries and reducing your risk of mental decline and dementias such as Alzheimer's.

MORE BRAIN-BOOSTING AND REJUVENATING TIPS

● Plenty of exercise for mind and body – keeping up the physical exercise will help you to maintain strength, flexibility and balance. And exercise your mind by reading, doing puzzles and watching challenging TV programmes
● No smoking – smoking adds to your body's free-radical load, as well as your cardiovascular risk
● Down with stress and up with fun – try to keep your stress levels as low as you can and make sure you allow time to meet friends. Get out and have fun!

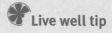 **Live well tip**
Watch your 'bad fats' – saturated and trans fats raise your levels of 'bad' LDL cholesterol, clogging your arteries.

5 SUPERFOODS TO KEEP YOUR BRAIN YOUNG

1. Tinned sardines in tomato sauce – for omega-3, and the phytochemical lycopene (in the sauce)
2. Broccoli – for folic acid and phytochemicals
3. Blueberries – for anthocyanins
4. Olive oil – for artery-smoothing monounsaturated fats
5. White tea – for polyphenols

'Monounsaturated fats, such as those found in olive oil, and nuts and seeds, help lower your "bad" LDL cholesterol levels'

 **Live well tip**
Replace red and processed meat with low-fat beans and lentils.

Recipes for mental wellbeing

The following recipes all contain nutrients which promote brain health and mental wellbeing.

SALMON AND VEGETABLE COUSCOUS
(Serves 4)
This can be eaten hot or cold

2 salmon fillets, grilled and flaked
150g/6oz couscous
1 tsp olive oil
1 medium onion, finely sliced
1 red pepper, deseeded and finely chopped
1 yellow pepper, deseeded and finely chopped
200g frozen peas, cooked
Ground black pepper

1. Cook the salmon under the grill for approximately 4 minutes each side, or until the fish is opaque all the way through (thick fillets will take longer to cook). Flake the cooked salmon and keep warm. Cook the couscous according to the packet instructions.
2. Place the oil in a non-stick frying pan and add the onion and fry for 5 minutes until soft but not coloured. Add the peppers and fry for another 3 minutes. Add the couscous, the flaked salmon and the cooked peas.
3. Season with pepper and mix together. Spoon into four bowls. Serve with a large green salad.

Health fact
The omega-3 essential fatty acids in salmon are good for the brain, helping to prevent mood swings and depression.

ROASTED STUFFED PEPPERS WITH CHEESE
(Serves 4)

4 large red peppers
2 yellow or green peppers
2 cloves garlic, finely chopped
Ground black pepper
2 tbsp olive oil
175g/6oz halloumi or feta cheese, cubed
50g pine nuts

1. Preheat the oven to 180C/Gas 4. Halve the red peppers, leaving the stalks in place, and remove the seeds and membranes. Deseed and chop the yellow peppers.
2. Place the red peppers on to a baking sheet and fill with the chopped yellow pepper. Sprinkle over the garlic and season with pepper. Drizzle over the olive oil.
3. Bake the stuffed peppers for 20–25 minutes until they have softened. Remove from the oven and add the cubes of cheese and the pine nuts. Return to the oven and bake for a further 10–15 minutes until the cheese has begun to melt.
4. Serve with wholegrain rice and a green salad.

Health fact
Pine nuts are a good
source of vitamin E.

CHICKEN WITH TOMATO AND ROSEMARY
(Serves 4)

1 tbsp olive oil
1 lemon cut into 8 wedges
4 small boneless chicken breasts, skin removed
175g/6oz cherry tomatoes
3 small sprigs rosemary
200g/8oz green beans
100g/4oz feta cheese, crumbled
8 pitted green olives, halved
Ground black pepper

Health fact
When the skin is removed, chicken is a good, low-fat protein source.

1. Gently heat the oil in a non-stick frying pan and cook the lemon wedges and chicken for 15 minutes, turning regularly. Add the tomatoes and rosemary and cook for a further 5 minutes Check that the chicken is cooked through, if not, cook for a little longer until the juices run clear.
2. Cook the beans in boiling water until just tender and drain. Add the beans to the pan with the crumbled feta cheese. Add the olives and ground black pepper
3. Serve with a green salad and crusty bread.

'Fruit and vegetables, packed with all those lovely antioxidants, have definite brain benefits, by scavenging the harmful free radicals that damage our bodies' cells'

Sleep

With our 24-hour lifestyles, getting enough sleep each night is often pushed low down on our list of priorities. But we all need a good night's sleep to give our bodies time to build new cells and repair damage to tissues, and for the brain to reset its functions so we will wake refreshed.

Some people profess to get by on a few hours a night, but they are the exceptions. Most adults need about seven hours' sleep a night in order to function at their peak.

Studies have found that insufficient sleep has implications far beyond feeling woolly-headed in the morning. Sleep deprivation affects our memory, judgement, co-ordination and leads to stress. Lack of sleep has also been linked to digestive problems and increased risk of heart disease. And it's not only the amount of sleep we get each night that is important – the quality of sleep matters as well.

Our diet (including the times we eat particular foods) is a key factor affecting how well we sleep. Some foods aid restful sleep while others keep us revved up way past bedtime.

Live well tips

Know what your bedroom is for – keep it for sleep and sex, not watching television. It should be uncluttered, cool and dark, so make sure your curtains are heavy enough to keep out the light.

Stub it out – don't smoke before going to bed. Smokers take longer to get to sleep and more often have interrupted sleep than non-smokers. Yet another good reason to quit.

Watch the booze – limit alcohol, especially late at night, as it can play havoc with your sleep patterns. It may help you to relax and get off to sleep, but will interrupt your sleep later in the night.

The best bedtime snacks contain both complex carbohydrates and protein, and some calcium, which some people swear by for restful sleep. Magnesium is also an important mineral for sleeping, so boost your levels by eating wholegrains and broccoli. Other examples of good 'sleepy' evening meals would be cheese and vegetable pasta or chicken and broccoli baked in a low-fat cheese sauce.

Keep your evening meal light and your servings small to give your digestive system less work to do before you go to sleep, and try to eat your meal at least two hours before you go to bed. Some people find that highly seasoned food interferes with their sleep, so if you're one of them keep hot chilli and curry dishes for lunchtime. Caffeine is a stimulant, so drinks like coffee are the last thing you want at night if you're looking to get a good night's sleep.

'The best bedtime snacks contain both complex carbohydrates and protein, and some calcium, which some people swear by for restful sleep'

Healthy Eating For Convalescence

When you're feeling ill, or healing after an injury, good nutrition can speed you on your way to recovery.

If you're cooking for someone who's poorly, remember they may not feel much like eating, so put the emphasis on small portions of tasty foods. Convalescent food should be tempting and attractively presented – not bland and boring.

Concentrate on unprocessed whole foods. Recovering bodies need protein to rebuild tissues, and vegetable sources like beans and lentils, white fish and poultry are easier to digest than red meat. Tofu is also an excellent food for convalescents, but it can taste rather bland when served 'plain', so liven it up with a marinade or serve it with tastier foods. Natural yoghurt is another good choice.

Good energy sources for recovery include brown rice and new potatoes boiled in their skins. Go easy on the fats (even the healthy oils) for a while, until the digestive system is feeling a bit stronger.

Fruit and lightly steamed vegetables are great when people aren't feeling well, because they're tasty, as well as being packed with vitamins and minerals.

Live well tip
Don't cook your veg to death – rather than boiling them until they're soft and sludgy, vegetables should be lightly cooked, to retain the vitamins.

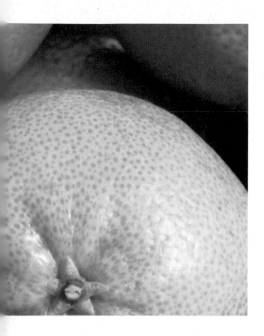

When you've lost your appetite, liquid meals are a good alternative to having to chew your way through your food, and are also easier to digest. Vegetable juices are a power-shot of vitamins and minerals, but fruit juice, especially orange and grapefruit, can be a bit too acidic. Smoothies made from natural yoghurt, fruit (or juice) and perhaps some chopped nuts and seeds are packed with protein, vitamins and minerals. You can also get convalescent meal replacements, which are fortified with nutrients, from your chemist or doctor.

It's very easy to become dehydrated when you're not well, particularly if a nasty taste in your mouth means drinking plain water isn't much fun. But keeping your fluid intake up can speed your recovery, so try tasty drinks like vegetable juice or diluted fruit juice, and fruit teas.

A non-alcoholic 'toddy' made from a big mug of orange juice diluted with hot water, and a teaspoon each of glycerine and honey, makes a wonderfully soothing drink for colds and sore throats.

VITAMIN C AND ZINC

Call in the healing vitamin! Vitamin C is needed for wound healing, for example after surgery. It's also one of the few things that can help beat the common cold.

Good sources: Citrus fruits, kiwi fruits, strawberries, cranberries, blackcurrants, tomatoes, sweet peppers, dark-green vegetables.

Zinc also helps wound healing, and boosts the immune system, helping it to fight back when it's under attack from bugs and germs.

Good sources: Beans and lentils, pumpkin seeds, turkey.

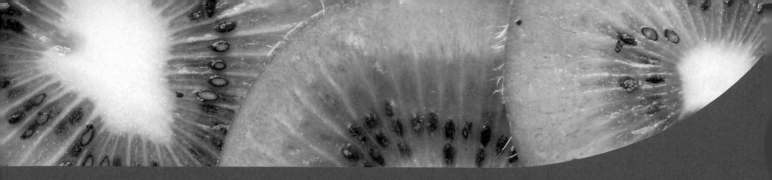

'When you come down with the sniffles, dose yourself with vitamin-C-rich foods like kiwi fruits, strawberries and citrus fruits'

COLD COMFORT

When you come down with the sniffles, dose yourself with vitamin-C-rich foods like kiwi fruits, strawberries and citrus fruits, and keep your fluid levels replenished with orange juice. Although vitamin C can't stop you from getting a cold in the first place, it can chase it off faster.

Zinc lozenges (allow them to dissolve slowly in your mouth – don't chew or swallow them) can also knock a couple of days off the duration of a cold. Be careful not to overdose – always follow the dosage instructions.

And a comforting bowl of chicken soup really can help a cold – the hot vapours help clear your airways, chicken provides low-fat, easily digested protein, and onions contain immune-boosting allicin.

Keep Active

The old adage 'use it or lose it' is certainly true. If you don't use your muscles, keep your bones strong and your heart and lungs in good order, don't be surprised if you become a little creaky as you age. You don't have to sign up for a marathon or bungee jump from the nearest bridge. You just need to keep active. And the great news is that, when it comes to exercise, it's never too late to start. Studies have shown that even people in their eighties can improve their mobility and balance by beginning a regular exercise programme.

Regardless of age, you still need both aerobic and strength exercise, even if it's not as vigorous as before. Find the right level of exercise for you – moderation is the key. Your aim is to keep fit, not train for the Olympics – exercise should be pleasurable, not painful. Walking briskly, cycling and swimming are ideal. You don't need to do all your exercise at once, you can split it into fifteen- or even ten-minute sessions.

If you've never tried them, now is a good time to think about taking up yoga or Pilates. Both are forms of exercise that not only strengthen the body but also improve flexibility, suppleness and balance – this is why they are so popular with dancers and people who do sport. It's also a good reason to practise them into your senior years, when good balance and co-ordination can help prevent disabling falls.

Live well tip

Walk right: If you plan to make walking a regular part of your personal fitness routine, invest in a good pair of trainers – ones that cushion your soles and support your ankles – and wear layers of clothing, so that you can strip off as you warm up and put them back on as you cool down.

Yoga

Yoga is an excellent form of exercise. You're never too old to take up yoga, and many people practise into their eighties and nineties. Yoga takes a holistic approach, stretching and toning the whole body. There are a wide variety of different yoga styles, so you're sure to be able to find one you enjoy.

Depending on the form you practise, yoga gradually improves your:

- Flexibility
- Suppleness
- Strength
- Stamina
- Balance
- Relaxation
- Concentration

There are many books, videos and DVDs on yoga but, particularly if you are a beginner, the easiest and safest way to learn the techniques is to enrol at a local class.

The most commonly taught type of yoga is hatha yoga. A class will usually be made up of limbering postures to warm you up, Asanas (postures), Pranayama (breath awareness) and a period of meditation.

Other types of yoga include:

- Viniyoga – a gentle form of yoga especially suitable for pregnancy and those suffering from a medical condition
- Iyengar – concentrates on precise movements and body alignment. Props such as chairs and bolsters may be used during exercise
- Ashtanga – this is more physically demanding and probably not the right choice for beginners. It is also known as 'Power Yoga' and postures and movements are performed in a continuous pattern at a quick pace

'Pilates, once mainly the preserve of athletes and dancers striving to regain fitness after an injury, has become very popular in recent years'

Pilates

Pilates, once mainly the preserve of athletes and dancers striving to regain fitness after an injury, has become very popular in recent years. Like yoga, it is suitable for everyone, regardless of age. Whether you want to tone your tummy, strengthen your legs or just de-stress after a busy day, Pilates has something to offer. It is considered one of the safest exercise techniques available.

Pilates is based on a thorough knowledge of the human body and works on the deep core stability muscles, gradually strengthening them without stressing the joints or the heart. Movements are precise, controlled and continuous.

Pilates will improve your:
- Strength
- Flexibility
- Co-ordination
- Posture
- Stress levels

BIG ISSUE –
Digestion

A happily functioning digestive system will help you get the best from your diet, enabling you to absorb the maximum nutrition from the food you eat. But a grouchy gut can not only make you miserable, it can also hamper the absorption of nutrients, laying you open to deficiency symptoms, malnutrition and a weakened immune system. You can eat the healthiest diet in the world, but it won't do you much good if you're not digesting it properly.

Probably every one of us has been affected by digestive problems at some time, and over a third of the population regularly suffers from digestive illnesses such as irritable bowel syndrome, constipation, diarrhoea, stomachaches, nausea and sickness.

The good news is that most of them can be prevented or relieved by what we eat, and when we eat it. Our lifestyle plays a part, too.

A healthy gut needs:
- Plenty of fibre
- Plenty of water
- Plenty of fruit and vegetables
- A good balance of 'gut flora', with plenty of 'friendly bacteria'

The last things it needs are:
- Stress
- Fatty foods
- Too much alcohol
- 'Trigger foods'
- Late suppers
- For you to be a couch potato
- For you to smoke

Live well tip
Eat little and often – If you gorge yourself on a couple of big meals, rather than several smaller ones, you'll probably overload your stomach, forcing open the valve that holds its top closed, and causing heartburn and indigestion.

Here's how to keep your gut healthy.

CHEW YOUR FOOD WELL

Taking smaller bites and chewing your food well prepares it for the next step in the breakdown process. Food in the mouth is mixed with saliva, which contains enzymes that begin the digestion process. When you swallow, food travels down your oesophagus to the stomach, where it's broken down further by digestive juices and enzymes. Small pieces of food, well chewed, are easier for the stomach to work on than big chunks, bolted down virtually whole.

Eating slowly also helps prevent the overeating that can contribute to obesity, as well as indigestion. It takes up to half an hour for 'I'm full' messages to reach your brain. If you gobble your food quickly, you may carry on eating when you're not really hungry any more.

FIBRE

Most of us need a lot more fibre than we're getting. We're advised to eat 18g per day, but the UK average is only two-thirds of this.

Insoluble fibre (from wholegrains, pulses, fruit and vegetables) bulks up the gut contents, and a lack of it can cause constipation. Gradually increasing insoluble fibre can also help in some cases of IBS. Don't suddenly increase your intake, or sprinkle bran on your food, as this can irritate the gut.

Soluble fibre (the kind found in oats, pulses, fruit and vegetables) is famous for lowering cholesterol, but it also feeds the friendly bacteria in the gut.

'The gut needs water (at least eight to ten glasses per day, and more in hot weather), particularly if you're eating plenty of fibre'

WATER

The gut needs water (at least eight to ten glasses per day, and more in hot weather), particularly if you're eating plenty of fibre, which needs to absorb water in order to do its job. Avoid fizzy drinks, as they can lead to wind and worsen the symptoms of IBS. Tea and coffee can also be a problem for IBS sufferers.

FRUIT AND VEGETABLES

Fruit and vegetables are high in both soluble and insoluble fibre, and you should eat at least five portions a day, preferably more. Aside from the effect of their fibre, fruits (especially prunes) also have a gentle laxative effect, helping to prevent constipation.

EXERCISE

Keeping yourself moving helps keep your gut moving too, aiding the normal healthy passage of food through the digestive system, and helping to prevent constipation. Also, stress contributes to many digestive problems, and exercise is a great stress reliever.

MAKE FRIENDS WITH YOUR BENEFICIAL BUGS

Your large intestine (bowel) contains billions of beneficial bacteria, called your 'gut flora' or probiotics.

These are the same kind of bacteria you buy in little pots of probiotic drinks and yoghurts.

How do they work? The probiotics don't have the bowel to themselves. There are some harmful bacteria in there too. When all is well, the good bacteria flourish, keeping the bad bugs' population down. But a poor diet, stress and especially taking antibiotic medication can upset the balance. If the harmful bacteria multiply so they get the upper hand, they crowd out the beneficial bacteria we need in order to stay healthy and feel at our best.

Probiotic supplements attempt to redress the balance, by boosting your population of friendly bacteria. If your gut is healthy, and your gut flora in balance, taking a probiotic supplement is unlikely to make you feel any better. But, if you suffer from a disorder such as IBS, probiotics are definitely worth a try.

When buying a supplement, look for one with the maximum number of 'viable organisms' – that's the living bugs.

Unlike the harmful bacteria that can cause stomach upsets, friendly bacteria also ferment soluble fibre from your diet to produce short-chain fatty acids (SCFAs). These SCFAs nourish the cells of the large intestine and aid healing of the gut, as well as reducing the risk of bowel cancer. And that's not all your beneficial gut flora can do – they also manufacture a small but useful amount of vitamin K and vitamin B12 that your body can absorb and use. So it stands to reason that you should give your friendly bacteria all the help you can.

You've probably also noticed products and supplements in the shops containing *prebiotics*. Prebiotics aren't bacteria, they're 'food' that helps the friendly (probiotic) bacteria to flourish. But the harmful bugs can't use prebiotics, so taking prebiotics gives your friendly bacteria a big advantage.

Another plus point for prebiotics is the fact that they're not a 'live' product. A disadvantage of probiotic foods and supplements is the fact that they have to travel through the stomach and small intestine, where they are attacked by acidic digestive juices and enzymes, and many of them are destroyed before they reach their eventual new home – your bowel. Prebiotics are unharmed by your digestive system, so they reach the friendly bacteria unaffected. Some foods have a prebiotic effect – bananas, onions and leeks are particularly good.

TRIGGER FOODS

Most of us have them – those certain foods that 'disagree' with us, leading to indigestion, gurgling noises and wind. Trigger foods can also contribute to IBS. For some people they're spicy foods, for others onions, alcohol or coffee. Fatty foods are a problem for a large proportion of us. The best solution is to learn your 'triggers', and avoid them.

EXCESSIVE ALCOHOL

Don't overdo the alcohol. Large quantities can irritate the stomach lining, and also hinder the body's ability to absorb and use vitamins and minerals. Women should drink no more than two to three units of alcohol a day, and men three to four units, with some alcohol-free days each week.

FATTY FOODS

As well as being 'triggers' for many people, fatty foods (such as deep-fried foods, creamy sauces and oily pastry) are the hardest foods for your digestive system to handle.

AVOID EATING LATE

If you go to bed and lie down too soon after a meal, stomach acid can 'escape' back into the gullet, causing heartburn.

STRESS

Stress appears to be an important trigger in many cases of IBS, and for many sufferers stress relief (such as meditation, yoga and relaxation) is the best way to relieve their condition. Stress can also make other digestive problems worse, as it interferes with the messages sent by the brain to tell the digestive system what to do. Think how worry about an exam or job interview can give you indigestion or diarrhoea.

INDIGESTION AND HEARTBURN – WHAT'S THAT?

A burning feeling behind the breastbone, or an acidic sensation that bubbles up from the stomach into the throat. It occurs when the stomach's acidic contents escape and rise up into the gullet, and sometimes as far as the mouth, where we experience it as a burning, acidic taste.

'Stress appears to be an important trigger in many cases of IBS, and for many sufferers stress relief (such as meditation, yoga and relaxation) is the best way to relieve their condition'

IRRITABLE BOWEL SYNDROME (IBS) – WHAT'S THAT?

The gut becomes oversensitive, and its normal functioning and the movement of food through the digestive system is disrupted, causing the gut to go into spasms. Symptoms include pain in the abdomen, nausea, bloating, wind, constipation or diarrhoea (or an alternation between the two), having to rush to the toilet, lethargy and headaches.

MEDICINES AND YOUR GUT

The side effects of some prescription medicines can include digestive problems, including nausea, indigestion, constipation and diarrhoea. If you have recently started taking medicine when you develop symptoms, speak to your doctor.

'The side effects of some prescription medicines can include digestive problems, including nausea, indigestion, constipation and diarrhoea'

TOP 10 TIPS FOR A HAPPY GUT

- 'Go brown' – switch to wholegrain products like wholemeal bread, wholemeal pasta, brown rice, oats, millet, bulghur wheat and buckwheat
- Aim to have some high-fibre food at every meal
- Snack on fresh fruit and vegetable sticks
- Cut down on fatty foods, especially fast food – too much fat isn't good for you anyway, and it's hard for your digestive system to handle
- Women shouldn't drink more than two to three units of alcohol a day, and men three to four units, with some alcohol-free days each week – more than this can irritate the gut and inhibit nutrient absorption and use
- Cut out your trigger foods – avoid spicy foods, coffee and fizzy drinks if they're a problem for you
- Learn to unwind – stress contributes to many digestive problems
- Make time for proper mealtimes and don't bolt your food – take time to relax and chew properly
- Don't lie down for thirty minutes after eating
- Don't exercise for an hour after eating

Think about . . .

If you're over fifty, and in the third Lifestage, you still need to think about the issues we covered earlier in this book, and consider how the food you eat affects:

- Your weight – do you eat more calories than you use?
- Your immune system – are you getting enough antioxidant-rich fruits and vegetables, nuts and seeds?
- Stress and fatigue – do you eat slow-release foods that keep your blood-sugar level stable?
- Your blood pressure – do you eat too much salt?
- Your cholesterol levels – do you eat too much saturated fat?
- Your cancer risk – how's your weight, and do you eat cancer-preventing foods?
- Your hormone balance – does your body get all the nutrients it needs to make these chemical messengers?

Now you've discovered the secrets of how to live well and longer, you can enjoy life secure in the knowledge that you are giving your body the best deal you can.

Continue with all the lessons you have learnt here and you'll maximise your potential for a long and healthy life:

- Eat well – concentrate on the tasty foods rich in health-promoting nutrients
- Avoid the less healthy foods that sap your energy and make you vulnerable to illness
- Find forms of exercise that you enjoy, and make time to do them regularly
- Relax and re-charge your batteries
- Maintain a network of friends and a satisfying social life
- Get enough sleep to leave you refreshed and allow your brain to do its vital maintenance work.

Do this, and you could add years to your life – and enjoy every one of them.

Index

Russell Hobbs, the brand associated with quality, innovation and style in the kitchen for the last 50 years, introduces three new products into the *You Are What You Eat* kitchen range. The range is designed to aid healthy eating by preparing and cooking food in healthier ways.

The new range comprises a Slow Cooker, which is one of the most convenient and healthy ways to cook a casserole, stew, curry or soup; a Deluxe Smoothie Maker, which would be a stylish addition to any kitchen and is ideal for creating healthy drinks for the whole family; and an easy-to-use Digital Steamer.

All products are designed in a crisp white finish with silver highlights and include a glossy recipe book to help get you started and assist you on the way to a much healthier lifestyle.

Products are available from major high-street retailers.